W. A. Lare, W. M. Hartzell

The Rebellion Record of Allegheny County,

From April, 1861 to October, 1862

W. A. Lare, W. M. Hartzell

The Rebellion Record of Allegheny County,
From April, 1861 to October, 1862

ISBN/EAN: 9783337213060

Printed in Europe, USA, Canada, Australia, Japan

Cover: Foto ©ninafisch / pixelio.de

More available books at **www.hansebooks.com**

THE

REBELLION RECORD

OF

ALLEGHENY COUNTY,

FROM

APRIL, 1861, TO OCTOBER, 1862.

CONTAINING

THE NARRATIVE OF THE ORGANIZATION OF COMPANIES AND REGIMENTS, THE PECUNIARY AID TENDERED BY COR-
PORATIONS AND INDIVIDUALS; THE HISTORY OF THE HOME GUARDS; THE OPERATION OF THE DRAFT
AND THE LIST OF EXEMPTS, AND MUCH VALUABLE MATTER RELATIVE TO THE SUBJECT.

W. A. LARE and W. M. HARTZELL, Publishers.

PITTSBURG:
A. A. ANDERSON, BOOK AND JOB PRINTER. DISPATCH BUILDING, Nos. 67 AND 69 FIFTH STREET.
1862.

ORGANIZATION

OF THE

Military of Allegheny County.

On the 11th of April, 1861, the Secession movements in the South—already endorsed by Legislative action in Several States—culminated in a demand by General Beauregard, commander of the rebel troops, for a surrender of Fort Sumter, in the harbor of Charleston. The refusal of Major Anderson to surrender was followed, on the 12th inst., by an assault on the fort, which, after a two days' bombardment, was capitulated, and the United States garrison, comprising less than ninety men, left the fort on the 14th inst. with the honors of war, saluting their flag. No loss of life had occured during the bombardment, but by the bursting of a gun in firing the salute two men were killed and four wounded.

The most intense excitement throughout the North followed the announcement of the attack on Fort Sumter, and on the 15th of April the President issued a proclamation calling upon the States to furnish 75,000 militia, to suppress the rebellion, and summoning an extra session of Congress on the 4th of July following. The quota of Pennsylvania, under this call for troops, was fixed at sixteen regiments, and the command of the Western Division of the State assigned to Brigadier-General Negley, for the purpose of organizing the troops.

The call for volunteers found Allegheny County, like all other parts of the State, almost unprovided with military organizations. There were in the two cities ten volunteer companies—the Jackson Independent Blues, Duquesne Greys, Washington Infantry, Allegheny Rifles, Pennsylvania Dragoons, Pittsburgh Turner Rifles, Lafayette Blues, Pennsylvania Zouaves, National Guards and United States Zouave Cadets—several of which had been organized during the military furore following the visit of the Chicago Zouaves, in 1860. In the county there were also a few volunteer organizations—the Pennsylvania Infantry, at East Liberty, Alliquippa Guards, M'Keesport, Turtle Creek Guards, Turtle Creek, two companies in Birmingham, St. Clair Guards, Union Artillery, National Lancers, and one or two others.

The greatest enthusiasm followed the announcement of the call for volunteers. Scores of companies were set on foot and tendered their services to the Governor. On the 15th instant recruiting began throughout the county, and on the 17th, the first detachment of Turner Rifles, eighty men, under Captain Amlung, left for Harrisburg. The remainder of the company, which was organized from the German Turner Association, left on the following day. On the same day, the Hannibal Guards, a company of colored men, also tendered their services. On the 18th, Trovillo's Invincibles, Robinson' Light Guards, M'Dowell's State Guards, and Gerard's Pennsylvania Zouaves, left for Harrisburg, followed, on the 20th, by a "second detachment," and Rippey's Scott Legion, Gallagher's Shields Guards, and Alliquippa Guards, of M'Keesport. On the 22d, the first regiment was organized in Allegheny County by General Negley:

Twelfth Regiment, Penna. Volunteers.

Colonel—David Campbell, of Pittsburgh.
Lieutenant-Colonel—Norton M'Giffin, of Washington.
Major—Alexander Hays, of Pittsburgh.
Adjutant—G. L. Bonnafon.
Quartermaster—James A. Ekin.
Quartermaster Sergeant—Samuel Walker.
Surgeons—Drs. A. M. Speer, R. M. Tindle.
Chaplain—Rev. J. J. Marks.

Co. A—Jackson Independent Blues,	Capt. Samuel M'Kee.
" B—Duquesne Greys.	" John S. Kennedy.
" C—Firemen's Legion,	" John H. Stewart.
" D—Union Guards,	" William Tomlinson.
" E—Washington Invincibles,*	" James Armstrong.
" F—Lawrence Guards,†	" Edward O'Brien.
" G—Monongahela Artillery,*	" Robert F. Cooper.
" H—Lawrence Guards,*	" Daniel Leasure.
" I—Zouave Cadets,	" George W. Tanner.
" K—City Guards,	" William H. Denny.

* Washington county.   † Lawrence county.

At the same time a battalion was organized of the companies in excess, some seven or eight, of which Captain T. A. Rowley, of the Washington Infantry, was elected Major. A regiment was subsequently organized at Harrisburg, the tenth company being formed of the men in excess in the other companies, and Joseph Browne elected captain. This was afterwards known as the

Thirteenth Regiment, Penna. Volunteers.

Colonel—T. A. Rowley, of Pittsburg.
Lieut. Colonel—John N. Purviance, of Butler.
Major—W. S. Mellinger, of Washington.
Adjutant—J. M. Kinkead.
Quartermaster—M. K. Moorhead.
Quartermaster Sergeant—L. Sahl, Jr.
Sergeant Major—Alex. P. Callow.
Surgeons—Drs. James Robinson, Geo. S. Foster.
Chaplain—Rev. A. M. Stewart.

Co. A—Washington Infantry,   Capt. David B. Morris.
"   B—Union Cadets,   "   John W. Patterson.
"   C—Negley Cadets,   "   Joseph Browne.
"   D—Washington Infantry, "   William Mays.
"   E—Fort Pitt Guards,   "   William A. Charlton.*
"   F—Rowley Rifles,   "   John D. M'Farland.
"   G—Taylor Guards,†   "   John H. Filler.
"   H—Butler Blues,‡   "   Alex. Gillespie.
"   J—Shields Guards,   "   William C. Gallagher.
"   K—Duquesne Greys,   "   John Poland.

*Resigned at York, succeeded by 1st Lieut. Hamlet Lowe.   † Bedford county.   ‡ Butler county.

A number of the companies which had already been sent eastward were collected at Camp Slifer, Chambersburg, Franklin Co., and others forwarded directly to Washington City. Those who reached Washington were organized into the

Fifth Regiment Penna. Vols.*

Colonel—R. P. M'Dowell, Allegheny City.
Lieut. Colonel—B. Christ.
Major—R. B. Petriken.
Adjutant—R. C. Parker.
Co. A—State Guards,   Capt. G. W. Dawson.
"   B—Turner Rifles,   "   H. Amlung.
"   K—United States Zouaves, " George Segrist.

*Seven companies were from Eastern counties.

In Camp Slifer, from the troops sent forward from Allegheny and Berks counties, was organized the

Seventh Regiment Penna. Vols.

Colonel—William H. Irwin.
Lieut. Colonel—O. H. Rippey, of Allegheny.
Major—Frank Robinson, of Allegheny.

Co. A—Scott Legion,	Capt. Maurice Wallace.
" B—Allegheny Rifles,	" Casper Gang.
" E—Allegheny Light Guards,	" H. K. Tyler.
" F—Pennsylvania Zouaves,	" Joseph Gerard.
" K—Pittsburg Invincibles,	" William H. Trovillo.

The Negley Zouaves, Capt. O. M. Irvine, were assigned to the 3d Regiment, of which Capt. Irvine was chosen Major; 1st Lieut. Lawson succeeding to the Captaincy.

The Alliquippa Guards, Capt. Snider, were attached to the 14th Regiment, Col. John W. Johnston.

While these companies were recruiting, the community was in a constant whirl of excitement. Public buildings, stores, and even private houses were profusely decorated with flags of all sizes and qualities. Private subscriptions for the benefit of individuals and companies were raised liberally —amounting in the aggregate to thousands of dollars. Revolvers, swords, bowie knives, sashes, and other weapons and military decorations were presented by hundreds, individuals, companies, and corporations vieing with each other in liberality. By the efforts of a few individuals, in some instances, whole companies were uniformed; but we regret to say, the materials and make, in some cases, soon proved to be of the shabbiest character. Thus several companies of the three months volunteers were twice supplied with clothing within a few weeks; once before leaving home, and again by the State, with "shoddy" suits, and both of such miserable materials as to fall to pieces before the campaign had fairly commenced, causing much needless suffering among the raw recruits.

During this period of excitement, the ladies took their full share of labor, sewing gratuitously for the soldiers, making lint and hospital supplies, and providing such delicacies as their means permitted. Hundreds of havelocks were made, but the discovery that the white colored stuff of which they were made had an injurious effect on the eyes of the rear rank men, put a sudden stop to the manufacture. Private subscriptions were raised to provide means both for the outfitting of the volunteers and for the defence of the city. Messrs. Knapp, Rudd & Co., of the Fort Pitt works, generously tendering the heavy ordnance for the purpose.

Departure of Allegheny County Troops.

On the 24th of April—eleven days after the President called for 75,000 men—the last detachment (excepting two companies) of the 12th and 13th Regiments, left for Harrisburg. At an early hour in the day the troops mustered and repaired to the East Common, Allegheny, where a grand review had been announced to come off. A slight rain had been falling, which increased to a heavy shower as the review was about commencing, and continued without intermission, interfering greatly with the Commanding General's arrangement for a grand demonstration. The review did not come off, the soldiers instead plodding their way, through the muddy streets and torrents of rain, to the railroad depot, which they reached in dilapidated plight, the column marching through Western avenue, Ohio and Federal streets to the river, across the Suspension bridge, up St. Clair and Fifth streets to Smithfield, thence to Sixth and down to Liberty, where three trains, consisting of thirty-three cars, were in waiting to transport them to the State Capital. On the route a beautiful silk flag was presented to the 12th Regiment by the ladies of Allegheny, and received by Capt. R. Biddle Roberts, of the U. S. Zouave Cadets. This demonstration took place at the house of Wm. Bagaley, Esq., on Western Avenue.

Before the troops reached the trains, the arrangements for supplying a comfortable lunch were perfected. A day's rations of bread and meat had been placed on each man's seat, and his tin cup filled with excellent coffee, most gladly welcomed by the soldiers after their trudge through mud and rain. In Kier's warehouse, near the depot, a table was bountifully supplied, and but few failed "to pay their respects" to it. Credit for this timely supply of comfort for the inner man is due mainly to the citizens who subsequently organized the Subsistence Committee, of which we will hereafter speak.

About twelve o'clock, m., the first (and largest) train moved off amid the most enthusiastic demonstrations, waving of handkerchiefs from the windows and housetops, and deafening cheers from the spectators, all cheerfully responded to by the men in the cars. At least ten thousand people had collected to wave farewell to the "gallant three monthsers." The smaller trains followed the first at brief intervals, and the crowd was not cleared off until long after the first car was out of sight.

The first train arrived at Huntingdon at half-past six p. m., and simultaneous with its arrival the soldiers were besieged by citizens bearing baskets of boiled eggs, sandwiches, crackers, cheese, hot coffee, &c. The second and third trains stopped at Altoona, and the men were there fed at the expense of the Government.

The trains arrived at Harrisburg between one and two o'clock on the morning of the 25th, and the men were quartered in churches and in the capitol. On the afternoon of the same day the regiments were mustered into the service of the United States, on the square fronting the State Capitol, on each side of which the 12th and 13th regiments were formed in line. After the ceremony, Gov. Curtin passed in review.

Col. Campbell's regiment, the 12th, left the same evening for "Camp Scott," at York, and Col. Rowley's left on the following day for the same destination.

At Camp Scott,

of which Brig. Gen. Wynkoop was in command, were the 1st, 2d, 3d, 12th, 13th and 16th Regiments, numbering in all about 5,000 men. Beside the Allegheny county companies in the 12th and 13th, another company, the Negley Zouaves, were in the 3d. The men suffered much for the want of sufficient clothing, which was not furnished for some time after their arrival at York.

On the 29th of April Gen. Negley issued his first General Order, assuming command of the 12th and 13th regiments, Capt. Leasure, of Lawrence county, acting as Adjutant General.

Major General Keim, with his aid, Col. Schaffer, of Lancaster, arrived at York on May 6th, and assumed control of affairs. Two days after, Captain

Ekin, quartermaster of the 12th, left Philadelphia, with requisitions for clothing and accoutrements for all the troops in camp Scott. He returned on the 12th, having been successful in his mission.

At this time, the bridges on the Northern Central Railroad, (destroyed by the rebels,) had been rebuilt, and trains began running regularly from Harrisburg to Baltimore, a special train going through on the 9th.

Gen. Negley, by direction of Maj. Gen. Keim, had added to his brigade (the Fourth,) the 14th and 15th Regiments, in camp at Lancaster. The Alliquippa Guards, Capt. Snyder, of McKeesport, were Co. K, in the 14th.

The subject of re-enlisting for three years or the war was now agitated, and excited considerable discussion. The question was not put to the men, and the reports that they refused to re-enlist are false. Being half a month in the service without equipments, when other regiments subsequently organized were already in the field, abundantly supplied with everything, the men of the 12th and 13th, were in no amiable mood. On the 3d of May, Governor Curtin was advised that there were three very fine regiments in Philadelphia ready to go into service, and was urged to accept them. They were accepted and at once equipped and sent off. When Capt. Ekin visited Philadelphia, he was informed that the 12th and 13th regiments were in excess, and that unless they enlisted for three years they would be sent home. The acceptance of the Philadelphia regiments had more than filled the State's quota of three months men, and hence the 12th and 13th, although fully organized in less than two weeks after the call for troops, were to be crowded out. But, through the active exertions of one of our Representatives in Congress, Hon. J. K. Moorhead, the Secretary of War set all things straight. Who was to blame for this trouble we cannot say, but it seems, through somebody's inadvertance or neglect, that the War Department had not been advised of the organization of the Allegheny county regiments.

On the 10th of May, (Sunday,) Gov. Curtin, with his Aid, Col. R. Biddle Roberts, reviewed the troops at York. Brig. Gens. Negley and Wynkoop appeared with their brigades.

The first instalment of overcoats and accoutrements reached York on the 19th, another on the following day, and from day to day until all the troops in Camp Scott were fully clothed, equipped and furnished with Camp equipage. The inferiority and absolutely rottenness of the clothing excited much comment and not a little indignation.

About this time Gen. Negley left York for Lancaster, to see after the interests of the 14th and 15th Regiments. His separation from the 12th and 13th Regiments, it was at first supposed, would be but temporary, but turned out that they were taken out of his command entirely, as he exercised no control over them from the time of his leaving York, and during the remainder of the campaign he had but one company from Allegheny county under his command—the Alliquippa Guards. This was much against his wishes, as well as against the desire, we believe, of a majority of the Allegheny volunteers.

On the 25th—having remained at Camp Scott exactly one month—the 12th Regiment received marching orders and was stationed along the

Northern Central Railroad, guarding it from the destructive intentions of the rebels. The regiment remained there until the expiration of their term of service.

On the 3d of June, the 13th received marching orders, and on the following day left Camp Scott for Chambersburg, at which place it arrived on the morning of the 7th, and went into "Cantonment Rowley," west of the town, in the Fair Grounds, where it remained a few days, removing thence, on on the 12th, four miles South, to "Camp Brady." Here the regiment was placed in the brigade of Col. Dixon S. Miles, U. S. A., composed of the 9th and 16th P. V., and detachments of the 2d and 3d Infantry, (regulars.) The 15th found the regiment at "Camp Riley," in Md., a mile and a half from the Potomac, and on the following day it was at "Camp Hitchcock," in Berkeley County, Va., two miles South of the Potomac, which river it crossed, with Gen. Patterson's army, at Williamsport.

Before daylight on the 17th, the regiment, with the brigade to which it was attached, retreated across the Potomac to Williamsport, and took up quarters at "Camp Miles," adjoining the town. Here Col. Miles and his regulars were detached and left for Washington City. The regiment remained at this point, spending the time most agreeably, until the 4th of July.

At the Ledger office, in Williamsport, some of the 13th boys printed a newspaper, entitled, "THE PENNSYLVANIA THIRTEENTH," dated "Camp Miles, July 4th, 1861."

M. Swartzwelder, Esq., having paid the camp a visit, witnessed the spectacle of a company parading in drawers. a supply of which they had just received. He was convinced, after examining a few of the pantaloons worn by the soldiers, that it was not the warmth of the weather that induced them (the men) to come out in clean drawers in the presence of spectators, rather than in pants which would not cover their nakedness.

As an evidence of the feeling concerning the "shoddy" clothing, the "local" of the "Thirteen" thus dilated:

"We advertise for sale a choice lot of rags, (material unknown) formerly put together as soldiers' clothing. If Mr. Neil, of Philadelphia, wishes to assist in a speculation, he will find his services appreciated by applying to the 13th Regiment."

On the day of the publication of the paper, and while Sergt. Maj. Callow was working the press, without positive orders the 13th crossed the Potomac the third time. Being short of rations, and directed not to move until his commissary department had been replenished, Col. Rowley formed the regiment in line on the bank of the river, and put the question to the men whether they would be content to live for five days on three day's rations. An affirmative reply was given, and five minutes later the regiment filed into the Potomac, while Doubleday's guns were belching forth salutes in honor of the day. Arrived in Martinsburg on the same day, (the second after the fight at Falling Waters,) and remained there until the 15th, when Patterson's army moved to Bunker Hill, twelve miles distant from Winchester. Here it rested in quietude, barring the nightly alarms, (caused by timorous picket guards) until the 18th, when the army moved, NOT to Winchester, as was generally expected, but to Charleston, in the direction of Harper's Ferry. Remaining at Charleston for a few days, the line of march was taken up for the Ferry, where the Potomac was crossed a fourth time. Encamping for a night opposite Maryland Heights, the regiment headed for Hagerstown, marching some twenty-two miles in nine hours. The men knew they were going home, their term of service having expired. At Hagerstown they took the cars for Chambersburg, thence to Harrisburg, arriving in Pittsburg on the 29th of July. They were regularly mustered out and paid off a few days afterward. So ends a brief history of the bloodless campaign of the three months men.

The 13th regiment, together with the companies in the 3d, 7th and 14th, saw quite as much service as any of the three months troops attached to Gen. Patterson's division, while the 12th regiment did most efficient service in performing the duty to which it was assigned.

The companies in the 5th remained about Washington City, and were among the very first troops which arrived to defend the National Capital.

The 7th regiment went from Harrisburg to Camp Slifer, near Chambersburg, and was assigned to the Brigade of Gen. Williams. It crossed the Potomac with Patterson's army, and continued with it in the marches from Williamsport to Harper's Ferry, whence the three months men were all sent home.

While at Charleston, the battle of Bull Run took place, and on the day previous the 13th was ordered to proceed some twenty miles in the direction of Winchester to burn some bridges and tear up railroad tracks, and had started on their mission. The order, however, was countermanded, while Capt. M. K. Moorhead, the Quartermaster, was endeavoring to procure the necessary tools.

The Alliquippa Guards, of McKeesport, Capt. Christian Snyder and Lieut.'s F. Shaum and George Haast,—attached to the 14th Regiment, Col. J. W. Johnston, of Westmoreland, remained at Lancaster for a considerable time, going thence to Chambersburg and participating in the campaign through the Cumberland Valley and Virginia. On the 14th of July, at Camp Negley, near Hagerstown, Md., the officers of the Guards resigned, because, as they stated, no provisions were furnished their men. The resignations were accepted by Gen. Negley, who appointed other officers, viz: Capt. Jas. A. Lowrie, and 1st Lieut. Alexander Forsyth, both of whom were on the General's staff, and the latter afterwards assigned as Quartermaster of the 14th Regiment, with James H. Snodgrass, as assistant.

The Negley Zouaves, of East Liberty, Capt. Lawson, also actively participated in the three months campaign, doing guard duty on the railroad at Hagerstown for a short time.

THE COMMITTEE OF PUBLIC SAFETY.

Pending the organization of the volunteer militia of the county, active exertions were making in the community in the furtherance of the county's cause. One of the most important bodies ever organized in the country was set on foot, and for months afterwards exercised a controlling influence in all military affairs in the county. The duties of the Committee of Public Safety were multifarious and laborious, yet they were attended to with a vigilance and promptitude that will forever reflect credit on the members. On the 15th of April an immense mass meeting was held in City Hall. Never before had so many persons gathered within its walls—never had the same unanimity of sentiment been displayed. This meeting adopted a series of resolutions pertinent to the crisis, the fourth of which authorized the appointment of a Committee of One Hundred, to act in all matters pertaining to the "patriot cause." This committee, which was announced by the venerable chairman of the meeting, Judge Wilkins, on the 17th, was composed of prominent citizens of all parties, and temporarily organized by electing Thomas Bakewell, Esq., President; John Birmingham, W. Bagaley, Hon. Thomas M. Howe, Wm. F. Johnston, C. Zug, and G. W. Cass, Vice Presidents; and T. Steel, C. McKnight, T. J. Bigham and T. B. Hamilton, Secretaries.

A committee appointed on permanent organization, at a meeting on the 18th, reported the following permanent officers: Hon. William Wilkins, President; Hon. Thomas M. Howe, Hon. William F. Johnston, William Bagaley, James P. Barr, John Birmingham and George W. Cass, Vice Presidents; Messrs. William M. Hersh, John W. Riddell, George H. Thurston, Wm. Woods, Jos. R. Hunter and Thos. D. Hamilton, Secretaries and Jas. M'Auley, Treasurer. The committee also reported the propriety of creating three sub-committees, viz: Finance, Home Defence, and Executive Committees, the organization of which, for obvious reasons, was not made public. The committees at once entered upon their duties in collecting funds and organizing the residents of the county into companies and regiments of Home Guards. The duties of the Executive Committee were of an extremely delicate character. At the outbreaking of the rebellion, there were in every community in the North numbers of residents who sympathized, more or less openly, with the rebels, and continued to supply them, for some time, with articles contraband of war. These articles were forwarded by railroad and express to points in the West, from which they could readily be distributed to the South. It became the duty of the committee to intercept these contraband shipments, and to put a stop, as quietly as possible, to the public expression of disloyal sentiments. For some weeks their labors were arduous, but finally resulted in a complete suppression of the illegal traffic. Hon. Wm. F. Johnston, Hon. Thos. Howe, Hon. Wm. Wilkins, Hon. John E. Parke, George W. Cass, George P. Hamilton, Thomas S. Blair, James H. Sewell, James Park, jr., James M'Auley, James B. Murray, William M. Lyon, Thomas Steel, William R. Brown, James Herdman, J. R. M'Cune, C. W. Batchelor, Wm. M. Shinn, William Phillips, Thomas Bakewell, James A. Hutchinson, H. M'Cullough, Reuben Miller, jr., Edward Gregg, Samuel Dilworth, William J. Morrison, Isaac Jones, M. Swartzwelder, William Coleman, Dr. George M'Cook, sr., P. C. Shannon, and Edward H. Stowe, formed this committee, of which William F. Johnston was elected chairman, and Thomas M. Howe Vice President, Geo. H. Thurston, Secretary of the Committee of Public Safety and J. A. Hutchinson, were appointed secretaries. Mr. Thurston, from his wide acquaintance in the community and his experience in business of a kindred nature, was enabled to be of great service to the committee in the transaction of its business.

At a mass meeting of citizens held some time after the formation of the committee, another committee was appointed to confer with the Executive Committee, being subsequently consolidated with it. It was composed of Messrs. B. C. Sawyer, A. C. Alexander, James M. Cooper, Wm. Robinson, jr., Wm. K. Nimick, John Harper, Robert Ashworth, Francis Sellers, F. R. Brunot, B. F. Jones, T. J. Bigham, John Myler, Wm. Semple, Jas. P. Tanner, Saml. Wickersham and James French. The original committee was in constant session for several weeks, day and night. The joint committee was chiefly engaged with business relative to the defence of the city. The last meeting of the committee was held on Sept. 16th, 1861, there being no emergency from that date until September, 1862, which required their attention.

The Executive Committee, or rather, the Committee on Munitions of War, Messrs. Jos. Dilworth, Geo. M'Cook, E. D. Gazzam, Jonas R. McClintock, and Robert Finney, on the 25th of April published a notice to shippers, to report all goods supposed to be contraband to the committee, sitting in permanent session. The Committee on the Transit of Contraband Goods—Messrs. George McCook, M. D., Henry Hays, E. D. Gazzam, Jonas R. McClintock and W. E. Fundenburg,—on the 28th, passed the following resolutions :

"Resolved, That all goods arriving at Pittsburg, and destined for Southern States, be stopped for the present, stored and insured.

"Resolved, That no packages whatever shall be allowed to go forward to Southern States till they have been opened and examined by the Committee.

"Resolved, That one or more packers be employed to attend to the opening of boxes and other packages and repacking the same."

The Committee still exercised a supervision over shipments during the summer. On the 28th of August, while the Collector of Customs was examining an Express car load of goods and munitions of war, a box of "friction tubes," used in firing army ordnance, exploded. Mr. James Batch-

elor, a brother of Captain Chas. W. Batchelor, Collector of Customs, who
was standing beside the car, had his leg broken by a splinter. Wm. Mc-
Laughlin, Expressman, John Maher, stableman, and Michael Regan,
laborer, were at work in the car. McLaughlin was frightfully lacerated
about the face and stomach, and one of his eyes badly injured. Maher was
also terribly injured, his right side being lacerated, his left knee laid open
to the bone, and his right arm, wrist and hand torn and mangled. All fortunately recovered. The cause of the explosion could never be clearly as-
certained, as the tubes are packed with extreme care.

The Home Guards.

Under the auspices of the Committee on Home Defence, preliminary
meetings were held in nearly all the wards of the two cities, on the 20th of
April, for the purpose of organizing a militia for home defence, and during
the fortnight following, organizations were perfected in almost every pre-
cinct in the county. Some of the companies adopted a cheap uniform,
others merely assumed a military cap, while a large number sought no
uniformity of dress or equipment. About the 1st of May, the Committee
were authorized by the State authorities to draw from the arsenal muskets
and rifles for the Home Guards. The arms were accordingly furnished by
Maj. Symington, and, together with a large number purchased by the Committee, stored in City Hall, which was placed under a strong guard for several weeks. Prior to the departure of the last detachments of volunteers,
1139 muskets and rifles were also distributed among them by the Committee.
As the companies of Home Guards were organized, they were reported to
the Committee, inspected and sworn, and on the 3d of May the distribution
of arms commenced, companies of riflemen receiving fifty rifles, and infantry
companies seventy muskets. The muskets were generally old "Harper's
Ferry" flint locks, but answered admirably all the purposes of drill. The
rifles were of the old pattern, without bayonets, but in other respects first-
rate arms. Forty-five companies were inspected on the first day, of which
twenty were supplied with arms. In the course of the ensuing fortnight,
all the companies organized were armed and under competent officers were
being actively drilled. On Friday, May 11th, the last company—the
Allegheny Grenadiers, Capt. Wray—were supplied with arms. The committee then reported a distribution of 2088 muskets and 882 rifles. Five
thousand five hundred men were organized into Home Guard companies.
Before distributing the arms, the committee required bonds from the officers
of the several companies. The organization, as might have been expected,
was made the target of not a little idle and malicious wit, and finally suc-
cumbed to ridicule and loss of novelty. Nevertheless, it had served a good
purpose in thoroughly arousing the military spirit of the people, and its
beneficial effects became apparent in recruiting under the subsequent call
for five hundred thousand men. The immense body, thus enrolled and partially drilled, made but one exhibition of its strength—in the grand parade of
July 4th. It had in the meantime been organized into regiments and brigades, of which we have the following record:

ALLEGHENY COUNTY

HOME GUARD ORGANIZATION.

Major General—William Wilkins.
Aids—John M'D. Crossan, John M. Tiernan, Mansfield Brown.
Inspector General—Thos. M. Howe.
Adjutant General—Jonas R. M'Clintock.
Quartermaster General—C. W. Batchelor.
Commissary General—William Bagaley.

FIRST BRIGADE.

Brigadier General—William F. Johnston.
Adjutant General—Benair C. Sawyer, jr.
Aid-de-Camp—Felix R. Brunot.

FIRST REGIMENT RIFLES.

Colonel—Samuel M. Wickersham.
Lieut. Colonel—T. B. Hambright.
Major—Jacob Britton.
Adjutant—J. H. Sarber.
Union Cavalry—Capt. Robt. Patterson.
Scott Rifles—Capt. Britton.
Second Ward Rifles—Capt. Mattern.
First Ward Rifles—Capt. Fitzsimmons.
Union Rifles, S. P.—Capt. ————.
Duquesne Central Guards—Capt. J. M. Roberts.
Park Rifles—Capt. C. W. Moore.
Eighth Ward Rifles—Capt. E. S. Wright.
Columbia Rifles—Capt. T. F. Lehman.

FOURTH REGIMENT.

Colonel—Joseph E. M'Cabe.
Lieut. Colonel———— ————.
Major—Andrew Burtt.
East Birmingham Guards—Capt. Cunningham.
Rich Valley H. Guards—Capt. Glenn.
Union Guards, Union tp—Capt. Frew.
South Pittsburg Infantry—Capt. Knap.
Dilworth Guards, Mt. Washington—Capt. Harper.
Ellsworth Guards—Capt. Duff.

Lower St. Clair Guards—Capt. Musser.
West Pittsburg Guards—Capt. Whipple.
West Liberty Guards—Capt. Espy.
East Birmingham Rifles—Capt. Dressel.

SECOND REGIMENT INFANTRY.

Colonel—F. C. Negley.
Lieut. Colonel—Wm. Kopp.
Major—J. R. Hunter.
Arsenal Rifles—Capt. Langdon.
Fifth Ward II. Guards, A—Lieut. Com. Wilson.
Fifth Ward II. Guards, B—Capt. Gangwisch.
Fifth Ward II. Guards, C—Capt. Felix.
Jefferson Guard—Capt. Hamm.

SECOND BRIGADE.

Brigadier General—George W. Cass.
Assistant Adjutant General—Robert Finney.

FIRST REGIMENT.

Colonel—William Phillips.
Lieutenant Colonel—R. W. Jones.
Major—J. B. Sweitzer.
Marion Guards—Capt. Sweitzer.
Howe Infantry—Capt. Bailey.
U. S. Zouave Cadets—Capt. De Barenne.
Koerner Guards—Capt. Holmes.
Bagaley Guards—Capt. De Zouche.
Kensington Guards—Capt. M'Candless.
Second Ward II. Guards—Capt. Appleton.
Ricketson Guards—Capt. Bell.

SECOND REGIMENT RIFLES.

Colonel—James B. Moore.
Lieutenant Colonel—T. B. Hamilton.
Major—F. Hambright.
Adjutant—B. F. Pettitt.
Keystone Rifles—Capt. Nimick.
Seventh Ward II. Guards—Capt. Ward.
Sharpsburg Rifles—Capt. F. H. Collier.
First Ward (A) Rifles—Capt. Hambright.
Shannon Rifles—Capt. Little.
Arsenal Rifles—Lieutenant Com. Pierson.
Allegheny Grenadiers—Capt. M. M'Gonnigle.
Steuben Guards—Capt. Lenhaeuser.
Harper Zouaves—Capt. Fullwood.
Fort Pitt Artillery, (five guns) Capt Metcalf.

THIRD REGIMENT.

Colonel—J. M. C. Beringer.
Lieutenant Colonel—James J. Larimer.
Major—John G. Martin.
East Liberty II. Guards—Capt. Gross.
Glenwood II. Guards—Capt. Cosgrave.
Swissvale II. Guards—Capt. Finney.
Wilkinsburg II. Guards—Capt. Semple.
Braddock's Field Guard—Capt. Smith.
Oakhill Guards—Capt. Baldwin.
Oakland Guards—Capt. Brown.
Versailles Tp. Guards—Capt. Shaw.
Penn Tp. II. Guards—Capt. Beringer.

THIRD BRIGADE.

Brigadier General—John Birmingham.
Aids—C. Zug, James P. Barr.
Assistant Adjutant Gen.—J. B. Guthrie.

FIFTH REGIMENT.

Colonel—Charles G. Smith.
Lieutenant Colonel—James M. Cooper.
Major—J. W. F. White.
Leet Guards—Capt. Nevin.
Allegheny Greys—Capt. Boisel.
Anderson Infantry—Capt. Duval.
Twin City Rangers—Capt. George Thompson.
Cass Defenders—Capt. Bradley.
Washington Guards—Capt. Steinbrenner.
Ellsworth Infantry—Capt. Miller.
Sewickley Guards—Capt. White.
M'Clure Guards—Capt. Smith.

SIXTH REGIMENT.

Colonel—Matthew I. Stewart.
Lieutenant Colonel—A. G. M'Quade.
Major—S. K. Rogers.
Madison Guards—Capt. Stewart.
Duquesne Guards—Capt. Jenkins.
Duquesne Cadets—Capt. Williams.
Shaler Home Guards—Capt. Lloyd.
Keystone Home Guards, Indiana tp—Capt. Robinson.
Duquesne Home Guards—Capt. Suttler.
Third Ward (Ally.) Home Guards—Capt. Mohl.
Allegheny Zouave Cadets—Capt. William Griswell.

THE RESERVE CORPS.

In the excitement which followed the call for seventy-five thousand militia, a sufficient number of organizations were set on foot to have furnished that number from Pennsylvania alone. Notwithstanding the fact that the State quota was filled in less than a week, these organizations—to the number of over forty in Allegheny county alone—still held together, though in many instances at great inconvenience to the men and cost to the officers. Strenuous efforts were made to induce the State authorities to accept these companies, and on the 27th of April the Governor decided to form a Camp at Pittsburgh. The temporary control of the camp was placed in the hands of one of the sub-committees of the Committee of Public Safety. The Fair Grounds were selected as a suitable site, and Camp Wilkins organized with Col. P. Jarrett, of Lock Haven, Clinton county, Pa., as commandant, Henry A. Weaver, Commissray, and Sam'l. P. M'Kelvy, Quartermaster. Twenty-six companies were immediately reported as ready to go into camp, of which we have the following list:

Government Guards,* Capt. Robt. Anderson; Fayette Guards,* Uniontown, Capt. S. D. Oliphant; Chartiers Valley Guards,* Capt. Charles Barnes; Pittsburgh Rifles,* Capt. L. W. Smith; Pennsylvania Rover Guards, Capt. Barr; Duncan Guards,* Capt. John Duncan; City Guards, B.* Capt. C. F. Jackson; Lafayette Blues, Captain Wilkinson; Highland Guards, Captain Robert Chester; Anderson Guards, Captain W. A. Anderson; Plumer Guards,‡ Captain A. Hay; Denny Guards, Captain H. Mackrell; Minute Riflemen,‡ Pine township, Captain Thos. Gibson; Allegheny Rangers,* Capt. H. S. Fleming; Independent Rangers, Capt. J. T. McCombs; Anderson Cadets,* Capt. George S. Hays; Pennsylvania Life Guards, Capt. Williamson; Jefferson Riflemen,* Capt. R. E. Johnston; Pittsburgh Artillery, Capt. D. C. Kemmerer; National Guards, B. Capt. J. Meyers; Pennsylvania Life Guards, Captain G. W. Leonard; Montgomery Guards, Captain M. Brennan; Anderson Infantry,‡ Capt. Alexander Scott; National Guards, A. Capt. H. Hultz; Irish Volunteers, Capt. John Murphy; Federal Guards,† Capt. J. C. Hull.

Great disappointment was created by the announcement, on Tuesday, that but six Allegheny county companies could be accepted and provided for in Camp Wilkins. An impromptu meeting of Captains was held in the Girard House, at which forty five companies were represented. A meeting was held on the following day, at which a resolution to disband was discussed and rejected, and a regimental organization determined on. On

---

* Subsequently admitted. † Now in the 63d P. V. ‡ Went into service in Virginia.

Thursday, twenty-eight companies, including a number not previously mentioned, were represented, and after some discussion two regiments were formed.

First Regiment : Colonel, Alexander Hay ; Lieut. Col., Robt. Chester; Major, Abijah Ferguson.

Second Regiment: Col., H. Hultz; Lieut. Col., John S. McCombs; Major, James Barr.

The Spang Infantry, Captain Scanlon ; Union Artillery, Capt. Large ; Turtle Creek Guards, Capt. Kunkle ; McKeesport Union Guards, Capt. Snodgrass, and Monongahela Blues, Capt. Blackburn, were among the new companies represented.

On Friday four additional companies, making ten from Allegheny county, were accepted and ordered into camp. They were the Anderson Guards, Chartiers Valley Guards, Duncan Guards, Allegheny Rangers, Iron City Guards, Garibaldi Guards, Anderson Cadets, City Guards, B., Pittsburgh Rifles, and McKeesport Union Guards.* As there had been no provision made as yet for a reserve corps in the State, the men were entitled, for the time being, to nothing but their rations. In the mean time the Erie Regiment, three months volunteers, under Col. McLean, took up quarters in Camp Wilkins, of which Col. McLean took command. A special meeting of the Legislature, in May, authorized the formation of a Reserve Corps, and provided for its maintenance until called into the service of the United States. Troops were ordered into camp from all of the Western counties of the State, until over three thousand men thronged its confined limits. It was soon discovered that the location was poorly adapted for a camp, and on May 25th Gen. McCall was sent by the Governor, with a military commission, to examine the surrounding country and select another site. Rapid trips were made to Sewickley, on the P. F. W. and C. Railroad, and Braddock's Fields on the Pennsylvania Central, and on the 27th the party, composed of Gen. McCall, Capt. Sheets, U. S. A., his Aid, Quarter-masters McKelvy and Benson, Commissary Weaver, Capt.'s Duncan, Dick, Barnes and others, and Messrs. James Henderson, James Gibson and Jos. S. Lare, proceeded to Hulton, on the Allegheny Valley Railroad, and examined the ground thoroughly, finally selecting it as a site for the new camp, which was named Camp Wright, in honor of Hon. John A. Wright, aid to the Governor. The camp was laid out on the 28th, on a broad field in the rear of the station buildings at Hulton, the ground sloping up to a steep eminence, about three hundred yards from the river. The parade ground was about one-fourth of a mile below, and fronted directly on the river. On the 30th, the first company—the Warren Guards, afterwards known as the " Wild Cats "—took up its quarters in Camp Wright, which was soon after filled,—by removals from Camp Wilkins and troops from other counties,— by over four thousand men.

IN CAMP WRIGHT,

toward the close of June, forty companies were collected, including the Erie regiment, while ten companies remained at Camp Wilkins. These

---

* Captain R. E. Johnston subsequently secured, by personal application, the passage of an act of Legislature for the admission of his company.

companies had nearly all recruited under the call for three months men, but previous to their muster into United States service were required to enlist for three years. In some companies a great deal of dissatisfaction was occasioned by the change, but all were finally sworn into service without the necessity of disbanding. In the beginning of July, the State officers appeared in Camp and organized the companies into four regiments, of which the Tenth and Eleventh contained no Allegheny county companies:

EIGHTH REGIMENT, P. V. C.

Colonel: George S. Hays.
Lieutenant Colonel: S. D. Oliphant.
Major: John W. Duncan.
Adjutant: H. W. Patterson.
Sergeant Major: Alfred T. Clark, jr.
Quartermaster: Joseph Fricker.*

Co. A. Armstrong Rifles,	Capt.	L. S. Cantwell.
" B. Jefferson Rifles,	"	R. E. Johnston.
" C. Anderson Cadets,	"	George S. Gallope.
" D. Brownsville Greys,	"	C. L. Conner.
" E. —————,	"	E. P. Shoenberger.
" F. Hopewell Rifles,	"	J. Eichelberger.
" G. —————.	"	J. B. Gardner.
" H. Clarion Union Guards,	"	Wm. Lemon.
" I. Green County Rangers,	"	S. M. Baily.
" K. Hopkins Infantry,	"	A. Wishart.

NINTH REGIMENT. P. V. C.

Colonel: C. F. Jackson.
Lieutenant Colonel: Robert Anderson.
Major: J. M'K. Snodgrass.
Adjutant: T. Brent Swearingen.

Co. A. City Rifles,	Capt.	L. W. Smith.
" B. Garibaldi Guards,	"	F. Hardtmeyer.
" C. Iron City Guards,	"	James Shannon.
" D. Government Guards,	"	Robert Galway.
" E. Chartiers Valley Guards,	"	Charles Barnes.
" F. Meadville Volunteers,	"	S. B. Dick.
" G. City Guard, B,	"	Brookbank.
" H. New Brighton Rifles,	"	Cuthbertson.
" I. M'Keesport Union Guards,	"	Wm. Lynch.
" K. Allegheny Rangers,	"	H. S. Fleming.

TENTH REGIMENT, P. V. C.

Colonel: John S. M'Calmont.
Lieutenant Colonel: G. T. Kirk.
Major: H. R. Allen.

*Since detached on signal service.

ELEVENTH REGIMENT, P. V. C.

Colonel: T. R. Gallaher,
Lieutenant Colonel: J. R. Porter.
Major: S. M. Jackson.

On July 17th the Reserve regiments were supplied with arms—altered muskets—and uniforms, and on the 23d left for Washington. The entire Reserve corps was formed into a division under Gen. M'Call, and during the winter quartered at Camp Pierpont, a portion of the division serving with credit in the battle of Drainesville. In March they were placed under command of Gen. M'Dowell, in his movement on Fredericksburg, and in June were transferred to the Peninsula, in time to participate in the Seven Days' Battles. They returned under M'Clellan in time for the battles under Gen. Pope before Washington, and were again in service in Maryland, in the battles of South Mountain and Antietam. In every action they have maintained their high reputation, and have earned their veteran stamp at a terrible cost of life. Since entering the service in July, 1861, the Reserves have been reduced from fifteen thousand to about six or seven thousand men. Gov. Curtin has recently submitted a proposition to the President to bring home these, and other veteran regiments, by detachments, for the purpose of recruiting their enfeebled ranks to their former standard.

THE ERIE REGIMENT,

one of the finest bodies of men raised during the war, was enlisted in Erie and adjoining counties under the first call for 75,000 men. As the companies were enrolled in widely separated localities, some time elapsed before the regiment was organized, and it was then too late for acceptance in the State's quota of sixteen regiments. Several of the companies were encamped for some time in Erie county, but on the organization of the regiment, so great was the reluctance of the State authorities to order its disbanding, that it was finally determined to retain it for State service, and it was accordingly ordered into camp at Pittsburg. The regiment entered Camp Wilkins on May 2d, with the following organization:

Colonel: John W. M'Lean.*
Lieutenant Colonel: Benjamin Grant.
Major: M. Schlandecker.
Adjutant: Strong Vincent.
Surgeon: J. L. Stewart.
Commissary: J. V. Derrickson.
Quartermaster: S. B. Benson.

Co. A.	Capt.	T. M. Austin.	Co. F.	Capt.	C. B. Morgan.
" B.	"	H. L. Brown.	" G.	"	D. W. Hutchinson.
" C.	"	John Graham.	" H.	"	J. Landrath.
" D.	"	J. L. Dunn.	" I.	"	Frank Wagner.
" E.	"	J. A. Austin.	" K.	"	J. Kirkpatrick.

Col. M'Lean took command of the camp, and of the companies subsequently ordered into it, until the transfer of the main body of the troops

---

*Killed at Gaines' Mill, while in command of the 83d P. V.

to Camp Wright, when Col. George S. Hays assumed command of Camp Wilkins. The Erie regiment was mainly uniformed, the liberality of the citizens of Erie supplying the means. The uniform was a showy and handsome one, and added greatly to the military appearance of the regiment. Prior to the transfer of the regiment to Camp Wright, great excitement was occasioned in the county and along the Monongahela valley, by a rebel raid, supposed to threaten Morgantown, and the regiment, together with one or two detached companies was ordered under arms, for the defence of the valley. The order was countermanded in a few hours, and the companies relapsed into their accustomed repose. It was transferred to Camp Wright, soon after the opening of that camp, and remained there for nearly two months, incessantly annoyed during that time by orders and countermands. During the "Morgantown scare" arms were provided for them, but not distributed, and the regiment was consequently never armed. It was never permitted to form a permanent organization, and at length Col. M'Lean applied directly to the War Department for acceptance. He was informed that his regiment would be accepted for three years, if ready to march at once. On his return, May 13th, Col. M'Lean announced the result of his mission, on dress parade, and the matter was taken into consideration by the officers. On laying the proposition before the men, however, a majority in nearly every company refused to enter service for three years. Many had enlisted for three months who could not leave their business for a longer time, but by far the largest portion were thoroughly disgusted by their treatment in camp. On July 19th the regiment was paid off and on the following day set out on its return to Erie, having spent three months in forced inaction. The regiment, as such, was never re-organized, but nearly all its members re-enlisted under the subsequent calls, Col. M'Lean organizing the 83d Pa. vols. He was subsequently killed in action, before Richmond.

The Unaccepted Companies.

It has already been stated that under the three months' call some forty or fifty companies were raised in excess of the county's quota, and that an attempt was subsequently made to organize these companies into independent reserve regiments. Under a heavy "outside pressure" Gov. Curtin finally agreed to establish a camp at Pittsburg and to order six Allegheny county companies into it. Strenuous efforts were made by all the captains to secure quarters in camp for their men, but out of over forty applicants only four were successful. Meetings of the captains were being held daily, and the selection of ten companies became a theme of angry comment among those not selected, or as they were afterwards known, the "Unaccepted Companies." Committees were appointed to wait on the Committee of Public Safety, on the Governor, and every one in fact, to whom the companies could look for assistance in their difficulties. The meetings were not always harmonious, and utterly failed in advancing the cause for which they were held, becoming at length merely gatherings for the purpose of venting contending views. The position of many of the officers was extremely trying. Some had recruited companies with their own funds, at the very outset of the excitement, and had supported the men, mainly at their own expense, for several weeks. Others who had made their appearance in the field later, had recruited companies and been ordered into camp, where they would at least be maintained without cost to the officers. This fact, especially, became a subject of bitter comment, and charges of unfairness and partiality were freely bandied by the unsuccessful. The selection of the ten companies, as may be supposed, had an extremely bad effect upon the "unaccepted" which gradually began to decline. It was discovered at length that no aid could be obtained either from the State authorities or the community, and the companies began gradually to disband. As already noted, a portion, embracing twenty-four of the companies, had been organized into two regiments, and a proposition was made to the Committee of Public Safety to maintain these organizations, if the community would furnish the necessary supplies and shelter for the men, Linden Grove being selected as a camping ground. The Committee declined to assume the responsibility, having no fund for the purpose, and the organizations at length yielded to inevitable fate, and disbanded. The last meeting of the captains, of which we have any record, was held on May 22d, and adjourned to meet at the call of another committee appointed to wait upon the Governor. Whether this committee ever reported we do not know, but as the companies were already entering the organizations of other States, it is not probable.

Had any concerted effort been made at this time by the community, there is no doubt that two or three regiments might have been maintained at comparatively trifling cost, until required under the second requisition for volunteer troops. Gov. Curtin, although he had recommended the formation of a reserve corps, refused to sanction the formation of companies for such an organization, until forced to do so by popular opinion. In New York, on the contrary, Gen. Sickles' brigade was established, although volunteers came in so slowly from the State that companies from other States were willingly accepted. Western Virginia too, which was just beginning to assert its loyalty, found the mustering of the State quota of volunteers extremely difficult, and at length established a camp on Wheeling Island, to which volunteers from all the surrounding States were invited.

In the meantime it had become apparent that the rebellion could not be put down in three months, nor by seventy-five thousand men, and the loyal community anxiously awaited a second call. Among the independent organizations and unaccepted companies, the subject of a three years enlistment had already been broached, and was generally concurred in.

The two independent regiments formed of the unaccepted companies of Allegheny county were pledged to three years' enlistment, if taken into Government service. The inducements held out by Virginia and New York, at length proved too strong for the companies so anxiously awaiting employment at Pittsburg, and men began to leave by squads, and finally by companies for Wheeling.

On May 14th the first squad of thirty men left for Camp Carlile, on Wheeling Island. It was subsequently announced that all companies would rendezvous at Wellsville, and on Virginia soil re-organize as Virginia companies, by re-electing their officers.

On the 9th, fifty volunteers from different companies, some of them disbanded, followed to Wheeling and entered Virginia companies. On the 22nd, the Spang Infantry, Captain Scanlon, and Woods Guards, Captain Hays, left for Wheeling, followed on May 2nd by the Jackson Guards, Captain Flesher. The Plummer Guards, Captain John D. Owens, (now Lieut. Col. 139th Pa., Vols.,) a company exclusively organized and uniformed by Jos. Plummer, Esq., of this city, started for Camp Carlile on June 5th, in company with the Anderson Infantry, Capt. Alexander Scott, subsequently known as the Belmont Guards. The Firemen Zouaves were organized in Camp Carlile on June 10th, by Capt. Robt. Gibson. On the 6th and 7th of June, the Friend Rifles, Capt. Brunn, a company organized and uniformed by Porter R. Friend, Esq., and the U. S. Zouave Cadets, Co. B., under Captain John P. Glass, left for New York, where they were subsequently organized in the Sickel's Excelsior Brigade—the former as Co. A., 3d regiment, and the latter as Co. A., 5th regiment. A few days after the arrival of the companies in New York, two members of the Zouaves, Lieutenants Ahl and W. W. Wattles, returned and organized Co. C. of the Cadets, which left for New York on the 21st of June. Under the auspices of Captain Brunn, a second company of Friend Rifles was also recruited in a few days, and left under command of Capt. Alex. Hay, for New York, on the 21st, in company with Co. C., of the Zouaves. Some difficulty took place on their arrival in New York, and the two companies, or the major portion of them, returned to Philadelphia, and were organized in the celebrated Geary's Regiment, since claimed as a " Philadelphia organization," exclusively.

The Pittsburgh Independent Scouts, Captain Anderson, started on the 20th of June for Reading, where they were incorporated in a cavalry regiment.

The falling off of men to join the reserve companies in Camp Wilkins, and those who entered service in New York and Virginia regiments, so reduced the unaccepted companies which still retained their organization as to render their disbanding an imperative necessity. One of the first companies disbanded—the Pennsylvania Life Guards—had already cost Captain Williams for maintenance $600.

Circumstances have since shown what a fatal blunder was committed in allowing these companies to enter the service of other States, without making any provision for their recognition by the authorities of Pennsylvania. Many hundreds of men left the county in organized companies, and there can be no doubt that nearly an equal number left singly or in small detachments and entered companies formed in other States, thus leaving no trace whatever of their military service. The neglect of the county to provide an efficient organization and to furnish support to the "Unaccepted Companies" has reduced the list of troops furnished, on which it has relied to avoid a draft, nearly three thousand men. A carefully prepared list of the companies which entered the service outside of Allegheny county regiments shows but eight or ten infantry companies—including those of Captains West, Ewing, Gibson, and Scott in the 2nd Virginia.

The Clothing Fraud.

No history of the "three months' campaign" would be complete without a record of the celebrated "clothing fraud case." It will be remembered that on the outbreak of the rebellion there was on hand in the country but a small supply of "military goods," such as heavy blue cloth for uniforms, blankets and shoes. In purchasing supplies for the State troops it became necessary, therefore, to adopt a different standard of goods, and in the haste requisite to fit out the quota of Pennsylvania immediately, the ordinary routine of advertising for proposals was abandoned, opening a wide field for corruption and rascality. The troops had been but a few weeks in camp, after receiving their uniforms and equipments from the State, until complaints became rife of the miserable quality of the clothing and shoes. Many of the suits furnished were so rotten and poorly made up that they fell to pieces in a few days, putting the wearers to the most absurd shifts to cover their nakedness. Shoes were found to have been constructed with an "insole" of shavings or wood, and so slightly put together that the outer sole would part company on the first day's wear. The blouses were made up of materials so loosely woven as to resemble in some respects bolting cloth, and decidedly better fitted for sifting grain than protecting the wearers from the inclemency of the weather. The material used used for this clothing was that generally known in trade as shoddy, a stuff made up by machinery from old woolen cloth. On May 21st, the first exposition of the frauds connected with these clothing contracts appeared in the Philadelphia Inquirer. A bill for $22,585 had been presented by Frowenfield & Bros., of Pittsburg, who had obtained a contract for a large number of uniforms through an individual named Charles M. Neal, an "Agent" for the State of Pennsylvania, and on whose endorsement the bill was "passed." The bill read as follows:

2,085 uniforms at $10,	- - - -	$20,850
347 pairs of pantaloons at $5,	- - -	1,735
		$22,585

The "uniforms" spoken of included, it is supposed, a coat or "blouse" and pantaloons, though the separate charge throws some doubt on the last item. Subsequent inquiry has utterly failed to show by what authority Mr. Neal acted in this matter, as Gov. Curtin entirely repudiated any "agencies" save those legitimately appointed—Quartermaster General Hale and Commissary General Irvin. The quality of the goods for which these enormous charges were made, and the relation of Mr. Neal to the contract were afterwards fully shown by legal investigation.

We have already noticed the operations of the Executive Committee of the Committee of Public Safety, and soon after this statement was published, an investigation was commenced by the Committee. On Tuesday, May 28th, M. Swartzwelder, Esq., at a meeting of the committee offered a preamble and resolutions, alluding to the charges of fraud in general circulation, and providing for the appointment of a committee to investigate the charges. The resolutions were adopted, and the following committee appointed: M. Swartzwelder, Esq., Thos. Bakewell, Esq., Hon. Wm. F. Johnston, and Wm. M. Shinn, Esq.

This committee addressed a note to the Messrs. Frowenfeld inviting their attendance at the examination, on Wednesday, May 29th, but as neither of them appeared, the committee sent a second note by Mr. Riddle, one of the Mayor's police. To this note an insolent reply was returned, that the parties accused would have nothing to say, and an intimation that the bearer of the note would be shown the door. Messrs. Frowenfeld had a few days before published a note in relation to the charges made against them, and requested a public investigation; as they now refused to appear, the Committee proceeded without them. They examined but five witnesses, on whose statements the matter was brought before the Grand Jury on Tuesday, June 4th. M. Swartzwelder, Esq. and Thos. Williams, Esq., were retained as prosecuting counsel.

The Court met on June 3d, and the Grand Jury organized, after an able charge from Judge M'Clure, in which the rascality of contractors was severely commented on, and the jury charged to regard the furnishing of improper food or rotten clothes as giving aid and comfort to the enemy. On Monday, June 25th, Mr. Marshall, counsel for the Frowenfeld's, moved for a continuance of the case until the next term of Court. Messrs. Thos. Williams, M. Swartzwelder and J. H. Miller appeared for the Commonwealth, and Hon. Chas. Shaler, Thos. M. Marshall, F. H. Collier; S. W. Black, J. M. Kirkpatrick, Jno. Mellon, and John Coyle, Esqs., for the defence. The case was argued on the same day, on the ground that Alfred Slade, J. N. Shannon and Jos. Lee, material witnesses for the defendants, were absent. The Court withheld a decision until the Monday following, when, the docket having been meantime cleared, the case was taken up, and two of the "necessary witnesses" were brought into Court. The third proved to be of no importance. Neal's bail had been forfeited, but was now renewed by his counsel, Mr. Brewster, of Philadelphia. To the intense surprise of the community, the case was here closed by a certiorari to the Supreme Court, and an allocatur from Judge Lowrie, the defendants having sworn that the President Judge was so far prejudiced against them that they could not obtain justice. Such a grave impeachment of the venerable and upright Judge of the Quarter Sessions Court as was contained in this affidavit, should never have obtained credence from the Supreme Court, and the surprise of the prosecuting attorneys may well be pardoned. A rule to show cause why the certiorari should not be rescinded was argued before the Supreme Court on July 2nd, and the case was regularly transferred to the Supreme Court, and a hearing fixed for the first Monday in September. At this time a continuance was asked by the Commonwealth, Sylvester W. Murphy, a clerk of the Frowenfeld's, and a very important witness, inasmuch as the prosecution was in a great measure based on his testimony before the Grand Jury, being absent. The case was continued til the 18th inst. On that date, Murphy being still absent, a nolle pros was entered, with the intention of entering a new bill on the re-appearance of the witness. Murphy was subsequently arrested in Philadelphia, on his return from his trip to Europe, but this extraordinary case was never tried, although the fact that the suits were not worth half the money charged was well substantiated. Their estimated cost was $7,00; actual value for wear $00.

THE SECOND REQUISITION.

FIVE HUNDRED THOUSAND VOLUNTEERS.

One of the most important acts of the special session of Congress called by Mr. Lincoln, was to authorize the President to accept the services of 500,000 volunteers for three years. Under this act, arrangements were made at once for re-organizing the three months' regiments then in the field. Unfortunately, the experience of the Pennsylvania troops had not been such as to induce them to favor the project. Many were utterly disgusted with the organization of their companies and regiments, scores of men holding commissions as field and line officers who were wholly unfit for the positions they occupied. Many were so dissipated that during the entire campaign their commands derived no benefit whatever from their instructions. Others were dissatisfied with the treatment they had received at the hands of the State authorities. Towards the close of their term of service, the general management of the State quota was greatly improved, but the rotten clothes, and still worse, the rotten food, supplied at the outset of the campaign, were still fresh in the memories of the outraged troops. The principal objection, however, originated no doubt in the utterly idle and unprofitable character of the campaign just closing. For nearly three months, the men had lain idly in camps or had been fruitlessly marched and countermarched until completely worn down. We have already given in detail the campaign of the four regiments in which the Allegheny companies were organized, and an ample illustration of all of these causes of complaint will be found in this brief sketch.

As we have already noted, the troops composing the Allegheny county quota reached home on the 29th of July, and 1st of August, scattered detachment detachments having arrived during the previous week. The reserve regiments had been sent to Washington a few days previous, but the city was by no means cleared of military.

On the 29th, a camp for regular cavalry was established at Linden Grove, under Colonel Emory, and several of the unaccepted companies which had maintained their organization were pressing forward.

On the arrival of the disbanded three months men, recruiting offices were at once established, and after a few days of comparative quiet, recruiting proceeded almost as briskly as in the earlier days of the war excitement, although men were already beginning to thoroughly comprehend the trials of the service and the magnitude of the task before the Government.

On the 25th of July, Gen. Geo. B. M'Clellan—who up till a few days previous had held a comparatively unimportant command in Western Virginia, and had been called to Washington to assume the task of reorganizing the army—passed through the city. He was received at the Allegheny Station by an immense crowd, and was escorted to the Monongahela House by the Twin City Rangers, Capt. Geo. Thompson, and Allegheny Greys, Capt. Boisol. Nearly all the Home Guard companies in the two cities were in the line of procession, which was closed by the companies composing the Fire Department. The Fort Pitt battery, divided into two sections and stationed on Cliff street and Seminary Hill, fired a Major General's salute on his arrival. At the Monongahela House he was welcomed by Judge Shannon, and replied briefly. Col. Saml. W. Black, who had returned a short time previous from Nebraska, of which territory he had been Governor, also made an eloquent address, closing the ceremonies of one of the most brilliant and enthusiastic receptions ever given by the city.

On the 23d inst. an immense mass meeting was held in City Hall, in reference to the proposed increase of the army. S. F. Von Bonnhorst, Esq., was called to the chair, and Thomas P. Bakewell and Rev. John Douglass were appointed Vice Presidents. Resolutions were adopted urging the collection of funds to aid in filling up the companies recruiting, and to provide for the families of volunteers, and the following gentlemen appointed on the Committee: Hon. T. M. Howe, H. M'Cullough, Esq., Dr. J. Carothers, Wm. Thaw, Esq., John Scott, Esq., and Alexander Nimick, Esq. The Committee set actively about the duties entrusted to them, and on the following week the recruiting of a regiment, to be under command of Col. Oliver H. Rippey was commenced. A regiment was already partially recruited for Col. Samuel W. Black, and Col. Rowley, of the 13th P. V., began the reorganization of that regiment, Lieuts. Foster and M'Ilwaine recruiting companies. On Saturday, August 3rd, the first three years regiment left for Washington under Col. Black. It has since been known as the

SIXTY-SECOND REGIMENT, P. V.

Colonel—Samuel W. Black.
Lieutenant Colonel—T. F. Lehman.
Major—J. B. Sweitzer.
Adjutant—Joseph Browne.

Co. A.	Federal Guards,	Captain J. C. Hull.
" B.	M'Kee Rifle Cadets,	" James W. Patterson.
" C.	Lyon Guards*	" Thomas B. Monks.
" D.	Finlay Cadets,	" W. C. Beck.
" E.	Reimersburg Guards*	" Thomas Kerr.

" F. Eighth Ward Guards, A. Capt. E. S. Wright.
" G. Kramer Guards,   "   F. C. O'Brien.
" H. St. Clair Guards,   "   Thomas Espy.
" I. Jefferson Guards,‡   "   R. B. Means.
" K. Eighth Ward Guards, B.‡ "   A. M'Donald.
" L. Chambers Zouaves,   "   S. R. Holmes.

* Clarion County. † Armstrong County. ‡ Jefferson County.

On August 21st the first detachment of Washington Infantry, A., Capt. J. Heron Foster, Col. Rowley's regiment, left for Washington, together with detachments of the Butler Infantry, Union Artillery, and Washington Infantry, B., of the same regiment.

On the 26th, the cavalry and infantry companies which had rendezvoused in Camp Wilkins, left for the East. The cavalry companies from Allegheny county were, the Union Cavalry, Captain Robt. H. Patterson; J. K. M. Cavalry, Capt. James E. Heron, the Moorhead Cavalry, Capt. L. Sahl, Jr., and the Pennsylvania Dragoons, Capt. H. P. Vierheller. The Infantry companies will be mentioned hereafter, as they were organized into regiments at Harrisburg and Washington. The National Cavalry, Capt. Boyce, from Upper St. Clair and Finlay township, left for the East on Aug. 28th. Detached companies were afterwards added to regiments at Harrisburg, rendering it a matter of extreme difficulty to follow their course. We give the organizations as far as we can obtain them:

ONE HUNDRED AND SECOND (OLD 13th,) REGIMENT.

Colonel—Thomas A. Rowley.
Lieutenant Colonel—J. M. Kinkaid.
Major—John Poland.
Adjutant—Joseph Browne.

Co. A. Washington Infantry, A.,   Capt. J. H. Foster.
" B. Union Cadets,   "   Jos. Bishop.
" C. Birmingham Zouaves,   "   Thomas H. Duff.
" D. Pennock Guards,   "   C. W. Enright.
" E. Union Cadets,   "   J. W. Patterson.
" F. (No name given,)   "   Wm. M'Ilwain.
" G. Johnston Cadets,   "   J. H. Coleman.
" H. (From Butler county,)   "   —— M'Laughlin.
" I. Iron City Zouaves,   "   O. M. Loomis.
" K. Vierheller Infantry,   "   H. Lowe.
" L. Rowley Rifles,   "   Jno. D. M'Farland.
" M. (No name given,)   "   S. L. Fullwood.

TWENTY-THIRD REGIMENT.

U. S. Zouave Cadets, Captain George W. Tanner.

TWENTY-EIGHTH REGIMENT.*

Colonel—John W. Geary.
Lieutenant Colonel—De Corpenay.
U. S. Zouave Cadets, Captain Thomas Ahl.

* Organized in Philadelphia.

M'Knight Guards, Captain James Barr.
Sewickley Rifles, Captain Conrad U. Meyer.
Elizabeth Mountaineers, Captain Copeland.
Fort Pitt Artillery, Captain J. M. Knapp.

FORTY-SIXTH REGIMENT.*

Colonel—John F. Knipe.
Frisbee Infantry, Captain W. L. Foulk.
Pittsburgh Rifles, Co. B., Capt. B. W. Morgan.

* Organized in Harrisburg.

FIFTY-SEVENTH REGIMENT.

Colonel—C. F. Campbell.
Verner Greys, Capt. J. B. Moore.

SIXTY-FIRST REGIMENT.

Colonel—O. H. Rippey.
Lieutenant Colonel—Frank Robinson.
Adjutant—W. G. Miller.

Co.	E.	Simpson Infantry,	Captain	Alexander Hay.
"	—	Marshall Guards,	"	James Calhoun.
"	—	Barnhill Guards,	"	J. H. Elliott.
"	K.	Pennsylvania Zouaves,	"	Joseph Gerard.
"	F.	Allegheny Guards,	"	Isaac Wright.
"	C.	Baxter Guards,	"	G. W. Dawson.
"	B.	Ellsworth Legion,	"	L. Redenbaugh.
"	G.	Lyon Guards,	"	H. W. Duval.
"	—	Walton Guards,	"	Charles Bryson.

These nine companies were subsequently consolidated into six, as lettered above.

SIXTY-THIRD REGIMENT.

Colonel—Alexander Hays.
Lieutenant Colonel—A. M. S. Morgan.
Major—Maurice Wallace.
Adjutant—George P. Corts.

Co	A.	Kelly Guards,	Captain	J. M. C. Berringer.
"	B.	Sharpsburg Guards,	"	William S. Kirkwood.
"	C.	Butler company,	"	Jason R. Hanna.
"	D.	Fire Zouaves,	"	H. O. Ormsbee.
"	E.	Etna Guards,	"	John A. Danks.
"	F.	———— ———,	"	Bernard J. Reed.
"	G.	———— ———,	"	Charles W. M'Henry.
"	H.	M'Cullough Guards,	"	Charles B. M'Cullough.
"	I.	M'Keesport Greys,	"	James F. Ryan.
"	K.	Hays Guards,	"	C. W. Chapman.

SEVENTY-FOURTH REGIMENT.

Colonel—A. Schimmelfennig.
Lieutenant Colonel— ——— Freybold.
Major—John Hamm.
Adjutant— ——— Becker

Co.				
"	B.	Turner Rifles,	Captain	A. Meckelburg.
"	D.	Kossuth Guards,	"	——— Schmidt.
"	E.	Alliquippa Rifles,	"	F. Blessing.
"	F.	Sigel Guards,	"	H. Amlung.
"	G.	Lyon Guards,	"	John Risser.
"	H.	Pittsburgh Infantry,	"	C. F. Lucius.
"	I.	Hooveler Zouaves,	"	John Hamm.
"	K*			

* Company K. was made up of the company of Captain Deiseroth, of Birmingham, and a Philadelphia detachment. There was one full company from Philadelphia in the regiment.

SEVENTY-SEVENTH REGIMENT.

Colonel—F. S. Stambaugh.

Co.	B.	Captain Thomas E. Rose.
"	E.	" ——— Robinson.

* There was but one Allegheny company, that of Captain Rose, in the regiment on its departure for Kentucky. Captain Robinson joined the regiment after the battle of Shiloh. Numerous squads of Alleghenians, however, are in the several companies.

ONE HUNDRED AND FIRST REGIMENT P. V.

Colonel—Joseph H. Wilson, of Beaver.*
Lieutenant Colonel—D. B. Morris, of Allegheny.†
Major:——— Hoard, of Tioga.

Co.	A.	Duquesne Zouaves,	Capt.	D. M. Armor.‡
"	B.	from Tioga co.,	"	Elliott.
"	C.	from Beaver co.,	"	W. Lowry.
"	D.	from Bedford co.,	"	Comfor.
"	E.	from Allegheny co.,	"	Jas. Chalfant.
"	F.	from Beaver co.,	"	Chas. May.
"	G.	from Allegheny co.,	"	Sprague.
"	H.	from Beaver and Butler co.,	"	Taylor.
"	I.	M'Farland Rangers,	"	G. W. Bowers.
"	K.	from Adams co.,	"	Kreitzman.

*Died near West Point, Va., on the 30th of May, 1862, of typhoid fever.
†Lieut. Col. Morris commanded at Fair Oaks, where he was severely wounded, and was subsequently commissioned Colonel of the Regiment.
‡Capt. Armor was promoted to the Majorship, and subsequently commissioned as Lieutenant Colonel, which position he holds at present.

FRIEDMAN'S REGIMENT CAVALRY.*

J. K. M. Cavalry,	Capt.	James A. Herron.
Young's "	"	J. Q. A. Young.
Faith's "	"	A. Faith.
Bagaley "	"	Geo. P. Vierheller.†
Keystone "	"	Benj. F. Blood.

*Afterwards commanded by Colonel James H. Childs, who was killed at Antietam.
†Resigned at Washington; succeeded by Capt. Williams, who also resigned.

LAMON'S BRIGADE, CAVALRY.

Moorhead Calvary,	Capt. Leopold Sahl.
Union "	" Robt. II. Patterson.

These companies, from Washington City, were transferred to Lamon's brigade at Williamsport. Hampton's battery was subsequently added to the brigade. Men were enlisted in the county for the regular service, in cavalry and infantry companies, and as marines for the navy, or for gun-boat service. Many Germans were enlisted for "German regiments," who were afterwards mustered into regiments raised in the eastern counties, or in other States. Of those who entered service in Virginia, we have the record of but five companies; of those who entered New York service, but two companies; of those who joined Geary's regiment, of four companies. The cavalry companies organized in this county were generally mustered into service in regiments made up from all parts of the State, but numbers joined regiments of other States, as those of Sahl, now Redpath, and Patterson, now Stewart, which form part of the First Maryland Cavalry regiment. It would probably be below the mark to say, that in addition to the 558 men reported as having enlisted from the county, in outside organizations, nearly two thousand have gone of whom we have no trace. The companies sent from the counties were not in any case, save the 62d, organized into regiments before leaving, though a tacit understanding existed in some instances, as in the 61st and 102d, ("old 13th.") The companies of Capts. Ahl, Ball, Copeland and Meyers were early consolidated with Geary's regiment, and participated in its entire campaign. It lay for some months at Point of Rocks and Harpers' Ferry, during which time it drove the rebels from Bolivar Heights. During the first campaign in the Valley of Virginia, it participated, with Knapp's battery. In the second advance from Harpers' Ferry it took part in the battle of Cedar Mountain, and in the subsequent battles under General Pope. On the re-organization of the army, it took part in the brief Maryland campaign. The companies in the 1st and 2d Virginia regiments, and those in Blenker's division participated in the entire campaigns of 1861 and '62 in Western Va., skirmishing, guarding railroads, marching and countermarching, and spent the winter, partially quartered and poorly supplied, on the mountain ranges. In the spring of '62 they crossed the mountains and joined the corps under Fremont. The main body of the troops enlisted here, however, spent the winter in the Army of the Potomac, surrounding Washington. Company's A, Capt. Foster, and D, Capt. Enright, were detached from the 102d (old 13th) regiment, on picket duty, under command of Capt. Foster, and lay for some months at Great Falls, Md., guarding the Chesapeake and Ohio Canal. During their occupation of "Cantonment Rowley," a paper was published regularly by the "Dispatch Mess," being a continuation of the paper published by the "old 13th" at Williamsport.

In March, the Army of the Potomac commenced its advance on Richmond, in which the 61st, 62d, 63d, 101st and 102d (old 13th) regiments participated. Several other regiments embracing Allegheny County companies took part in the campaign, from the taking of Yorktown until the siege of Richmond, the Reserve regiments joining the army just before the bloody seven days' battles. After the removal of the army from the Peninsula to Fredericksburg, the Allegheny troops were engaged in one or other of the actions during Pope's retreat to Washington. They were subsequently re-organized under M'Clellan, and participated with honor in the battles of South Mountain and Antietam. One company of Allegheny volunteers, under Capt. Thos. E. Rose, was organized as a portion of the 77th regiment, Col. Stambaugh, and embarked for Kentucky under Gen. Negley. They took part in the campaign of last Spring and Summer, were in the battle of Pittsburg Landing and at the siege of Corinth. They are now in the force operating under Gen. Buell. The Anderson cavalry, made up of representatives from all parts of the State, and one of the finest bodies organized in Pennsylvania, also participated in the Kentucky campaign as Buell's body guard, and in other special service. The names of those enlisted here for the original Troop were : Sergt. Frank B. Ward,(now Major in regiment;) Corporal Wm. T. M'Clure; Privates Wm. Strain, Robert Henderson, James C. Sproul, Henry J. Toudy, Walter F. Austin, John S. Murray, John E. Skillen. The Troop has recently been increased to a full regiment.

A full record of the casualties during this bloody campaign will not be made until the information is officially given by a publication of the army rolls. We find published the following names of commissioned officers lost in battle or by sickness; of the long list of privates and non-commissioned officers carried off by disease or the chances of battle, our space would preclude the publication, even could the information be procured.

1st Lieut. Alfred Wechsler, Young's Cavalry, died in Pittsburg, Sept. 8, 1861.

1st Lieut. Alfred Sickman, Co. G., 2d Va., killed at Cheat Mountain, Dec., 1861.

1st Lieut. E. R. Darlington, Co. A., 9th Pa. R. C., died at Georgetown, D. C., Oct. 21, 1861.

1st Lieut. W. J. Phillips, Co. L., 102d Pa., died at Washington, D. C., Dec. 11, 1861.

Capt. Leopold Sahl, Jr., Moorhead Cavalry, thigh terribly shattered at Slippery Creek, near Springfield, Hampshire co., Va., on the 4th of June, 1862, and died at Cumberland on the 17th, thirteen days after. He was returning from a scout with his company and fell into an ambuscade.

Capt. C. W. Chapman and Lieut. James M. Lysle, (Quartermaster) of 63d Regt., was killed while reconnoitering outside the picket lines near Pohick Run, Va., on the 5th of March, 1862.

Capt. Jacob Brunn, Co. E. (Friend Rifles) 3d Regt, Excelsior Brigade, killed at the battle of Williamsburg, Va., on May 5th, 1862.

Lieut. Mart. Miller, of same company, was killed in the same engagement.

Col. Oliver H. Rippey, 61st P. V., was killed at the battle of Fair Oaks or Seven Pines, May 31st, 1862.

Capt. Jos. Gerard, Co. K. 61st., Lieut. W. B. Kenney, Co. D., 102d, Capt. G. W. Gillespie, Co. B., 103d, Lieut. Scott, 61st, were also killed in the battle at Fair Oaks.

Col. Samuel W. Black, at battle of Gaines' Hill, June 28th, 1862. Body not recovered, and buried on the field.

Major John Poland, 102d P. V., and Lieut. Thomas Mooney, killed at Malvern Hill, July 1st, 1862. Lieut. Beatty, Pittsburg Rifles, 9th Reserves, was killed in the same action.

Col. Jas. H. Childs. 4th Cavalry, killed at the battle of Antietam, near Sharpsburg, Sept. 17th, 1862.

Capt. Jas. T. Shannon, Co. C., 9th Reserves, died at Washington City, on the 14th Sept., 1862, from the effects of a wound in the head, received at the second battle of Bull Run, August 21.

Recruiting Service.

Capt. J. Heron Foster and Lieut. W. B. Kenney, Sergts. Wilkinson and P. P. Baer, and A. P. Callow, of the 102d (Col. Rowley's) regiment, were detailed on recruiting service in January, 1862, opening offices on the 1st of February—Capt. Foster, on Fifth street, Pittsburg, and Lieut. Kenney, on Federal street, Allegheny. There were enlisted from Feb. 1st to April 10th, one hundred and fifty-five recruits, which were distributed amongst twenty-seven Penna. regiments. More than one-half of the recruits were obtained by Capt. Foster and Lieut. Kenney, although all the men enlisting with them did not join the 102d.

The second detachment of recruiting officers arrived in August, and are yet in the city. Capt. E. S. Wright, of the 62d, one of the number, was appointed provost marshal, and is acting in that capacity at the present date, having his office in Lyon's building, 5th street, removing thence from 67 Fourth street.

Relief Committee.

Soon after active recruiting commenced, in April, 1861, a number of prominent citizens called upon Gen. Negley and authorized him to publish the statement that the families of volunteers would be provided for in their absence, by the community. In pursuance of this pledge, meetings were held in Pittsburg and Allegheny, and under the auspices of the Finance Committee, of the Committee of Public Safety, collections commenced, and rooms were opened for the transaction of business. On the 15th of June the Committee was distributing relief to 570 families, and the number was considerably increased after that date. Besides providing for these families, the Committee, in accordance with a resolution of the banks, which subscribed $3000 to the fund, purchased 1800 percussion muskets. Many subscriptions of large sums were made by individuals and corporations, but our limits forbid a publication in detail. Sub-committees for collection were appointed in all the wards, boroughs and townships, and to these committees was entrusted the duty of hearing and determining upon applications for relief. Many of the precincts returned comparatively small sums, although their subsequent claims for relief were large. We give below the names of collectors and sums collected in twenty-nine districts. In the remaining districts the sums reported by collectors were small. The total amount collected, in cash, dry goods, groceries, etc. was $24,251 90, which was disbursed during the Summer. In cash $18,500, was distributed and in dry goods, etc. $2,200.

In the Autumn, the fund having been exhausted, the Relief Committee was organized as required by Legislature, and the county assumed the distribution of relief. The Commissioners, who had levied a two-mill tax and appointed collectors, subsequently revoked the appointments, recalled the books and borrowed the requisite funds. In order to meet pressing claims for relief, the two-mill tax not being paid into the Treasury for some time, $26,901 were paid out of the funds in the Treasury. For the year 1861 the sum assessed was $55,775. Under the Relief act sub-committees were appointed for each ward, borough and township, by whom the relief claims were examined and reported, and the relief funds paid out. The first relief rolls were presented in September, 1861. The tax assessed in 1862 was $54,927. The sum collected was exhausted in the first seven months of the year, and the last relief was paid out in August. The exact amount paid by the county is not known, as the accounts are not yet audited.

5

Collectors for the Volunteer Fund.

PITTSBURG.

1. Allen Cordell, Caleb Russell,	$ 3,500 00
2. Minas Tindle, Jas. M'Cabe,	2,478 25
3. Jackson Duncan, C. L. Magee,	198 25
4. C. West, W. H. Edmonds,	1,838 00
5. James Dain, B. Buerkle,	669 75
6. A. B. Berger, J. C. Cummings,	1,112 00
8. B. Preston, B. C. Sawyer, jr.,	413 02
9. James M'Cune, W. O. Davis,	843 43

ALLEGHENY.

1. Simeon Bulford, Saml. Dyer,	456 50
2. J. J. Moore, W. A. Reed,	151 00
3. John Swan, John Brown,	515 00
4. John Morrison, Henry Ansbutz,	868 50

BOROUGHS.

Duquesne, W. C. Miller, Lewis Felbach,	$ 37 25
South Pittsburg, Evans Davis, F. C. Jones,	100 00
Monongahela, Richard Peary, J. D. Hutzman,	209 64

West Pittsburg, David Edwards, G. Wettengill,	31 25
Birmingham, 1st Precinct, Daniel Berg, A. B. Stevenson,	436 00
" 2d Precinct, Danl Mc Cutcheon, J C. Shaffer,	1,019 00
Manchester, B. A. Sampson, Cyrus Townsend, jr.,	69 00
Temperanceville, Jno. Smitley, Dr. Simcox,	47 09

TOWNSHIPS.

Pitt, James Maginnis, Geo. Ewart,	$ 400 00
Penn, C. Snively, David Collins,	89 29
Lower St. Clair, W. Dilworth, Jos Keeling,	200 00
M'Clure, H. L. Bollman, T. Farley,	240 75
Wilkins, H. Chalfant, Jas. Kelly,	65 00
Versailles, Jno. J. Muse, Col. W. L. Miller,	23 25
Finlay, A. R. Brown, Dr. Pollock,	10 00
Reserve, Rev. A. D. Campbell, W. Neeb,	65 00

THE THIRD REQUISITION,

AND A

HISTORY OF THE DRAFT.

The third requisition, for three hundred thousand men, and the draft ordered for an equal number, may be treated as a single event, as but few volunteers were secured until after the second order was issued. In several states the orders were considered as a call for six hundred thousand men, and apportioned among the districts as a single quota. In Pennsylvania the recruiting of the quota has been so mismanaged that no definite policy can be said to have been pursued relative to it. It is quite probable that the governors were notified on the issuing of the third requisition that an order for a draft would follow, but no public or official notice to that effect was given, although rumors of a draft preceded the publication of the order several days.

On the 28th of June, a letter was addressed to the President by the Governors of the loyal States, requesting him to take measures for an immediate increase of the army. In pursuance of this request, the President, on the 1st of July, issued his third requisition, calling upon the loyal States to furnish three hundred thousand volunteers. In some of the States immediate steps were taken for recruiting the quota required, but in Pennsylvania the volunteer movements were proceeding very leisurely on the 21st, when the Governor issued his proclamation, calling for twenty-one regiments of volunteers in the State. He had in the interim secured an order for the acceptance of nine months, instead of three years volunteers, and of recruits for the old regiments for twelve months. Congress at its previous session had fixed a bounty for volunteers of one hundred dollars, one-fourth to be paid at the time of enlistment and the balance at the close. It had also sanctioned the payment of one months' pay in advance, making an enlistment bounty of thirty-eight dollars. In several States the Governors, in order to hasten enlistments, had added to this a State bounty of fifty dollars or more; but in issuing his proclamation Governor Curtin announced that no bounty would be paid by the State. The quota of Allegheny county by this proclamation was fixed at fifteen companies of nine months' men. Immediate measures were taken throughout the State to hasten recruiting, and on July 25th, in pursuance of previous notice, an immense mass meeting was held on the West Commons, in Allegheny City. At least fifteen thousand people were assembled and the utmost enthusiasm prevailed.

Four stands had been erected on different portions of the Common for the convenience of the crowd, and at one o'clock the meeting was organized, at the main stand, by the Committee of Arrangements, and the following list of officers announced:

STAND No. 1. Hon. Wm. Wilkins, President, assisted by a great number of Vice Presidents; Robt. Finney, J. R. Hunter, S. Harper, E. A. Montooth, Wm. B. Negley, W. C. Moreland, Thos. M. Bayne, and H. E. Davis, Secretaries.

STAND No. 2. Gen. Wm. Robinson, jr., President, assisted by Simon Drum, John Morrison, C. T. Ihmsen, J. M'D. Crossan, and Thos. M'Kee, Vice Presidents.

'STAND No. 3. Thomas Bakewell, Esq., President, assisted by B. C. Sawyer, G. L. B. Fetterman, John Birmingham, J. Sampson, and B. A. Mevay, Vice Presidents.

German Stand, G. G. Backofen, President, assisted by N. Voeghtly, Francis Felix, Major D. Fickeisen, Dr. A. H. Gross and A. Holstein, Vice Presidents.

Proceedings opened with prayer by Rev. Dr. Howard. Hon. P. C. Shannon then introduced Judge Wilkins who read a stirring address. Gov. Curtin, who was present on the stand, followed in an able but brief speech, at the close of which a series of resolutions were read and adopted.

The resolutions set forth the duty of loyal men to rise to the support of the Union in its hour of peril; the determination of Pennsylvania never to retire from the contest until the rebellion was crushed; calling on the authorities for an energetic employment of every means in their power to re-establish the authority of the Constitution; that the gratitude of the people of the State was due to Gov. Curtin for his labors in support of the Government; that a subscription be raised for a $50 bounty to volunteers; and that citizens of the county be earnestly requested to call meetings for the encouragement of recruiting. The tenth resolution provided that to raise the necessary funds for paying the bounty and assisting in preparing troops for the field, the following Committee should be appointed to collect and disburse:

Messrs. THOMAS M. HOWE, THOS. BAKEWELL, JAMES PARK, Jr., GEO. W. CASS, ISAAC JONES, B. F. JONES, WM. K. NIMICK, JOHN HARPER, THOS. S. BLAIR, P. C. SHANNON, JOHN H. SHOENBERGER and JAMES B. MURRAY.

The adoption of the resolutions was followed by a speech from Hon. W. F. Johnston, the audience having already divided to the several stands. Hon. Wilson M'Candless, Judge of the U. S. Court, Prof. S. J. Wilson, of the Western Theological Seminary, Rev. James Prestly, Hon. John Covode, T. J. Bigham, John H. Hampton, Wm. C. Moreland, Capt. John A. Danks, of the 63d regiment, Hon. Robt. M'Knight, J. R, Hunter and others also addressed the meeting.

The impulse given to recruiting by this meeting was quite marked. Companies for nine months and for the war were immediately set on foot in both cities. On the 28th an order was issued revoking the permission given Governor Curtin to recruit nine months regiments, on the ground that the time of service was too short to be effective, and that, as a similar privilege could not be extended to all the states, the discrimination would justly provoke complaint. The mustering officer was instructed to continue mustering in nine months' men until August 10th, and on that date the time was extended, to permit regiments already formed to recruit to the regular standard, until the 23d inst. In the interval thus allowed a sufficient number of companies were organized in Allegheny county to fill its quota under the first call. At the same time the recruiting of three years' men was rapidly progressing. In Allegheny city an impetus was given to the nine months' enlistments by the organization of the "Clark Infantry," a company under Rev. J. B. Clark, a clergyman of the 2nd United Presbyterian Church, in that city. Scores of men whose dread of the irreligious surroundings of the soldier had deterred them from enlisting, rushed to his standard, and his company was soon filled to overflowing. A second, third and fourth—one under command of the Mayor of the city, Simon Drum, Esq.—were organized in a few days, and on the date fixed by the Government a regiment was organized, of which Captain Clark was elected Colonel. Three years companies were also being organized, and under the auspices of William M. Semple, of Allegheny, the Semple Infantry was organized by William H. Moody, a similar "rush" resulting in the formation of four companies. We may here remark that no man in the community has displayed a more genuine spirit of liberality than Mr. Semple, who in donations to the companies bearing his name and in other forms has expended nearly $3000 towards the formation and equipment of the 139th regiment. Edward J. Allen, well known as the author of the "Oregon Trail," which appeared in the Daily Dispatch some years ago, also set about the organization of an Engineer regiment, which was subsequently, we believe, mustered into service as Infantry. The organization of these regiments will be given below:

ONE HUNDRED AND TWENTY-THIRD REGIMENT.

Colonel—John B. Clark.
Lieutenant Colonel—F. Gast.
Major—H. Danver.

Co.				
"	A.	Cass Infantry,	Captain	F. Gast.
"	B.	Butchers Infantry,	"	H. Danver.
"	C.	Clark Infantry, A.,	"	J. B. Clark.
"	D.	Walker Infantry, B.,	"	H. K. Tyler.
"	E.	Clark Infantry, B.	"	D. Boisel.
"	F.	Tarentum Infantry,	"	J. Boyd.
"	G.	Powers' Infantry,	"	R. Humes.
"	H.	Clark Infantry, C.,	"	S. Drum.
"	I.	Howe Engineers,	"	D. E. Adams.
"	K.	Watt and Butchers Infantry	"	H. Maxwell.

ONE HUNDRED AND THIRTY-SIXTH REGIMENT.

Colonel—Thomas M. Bayne, of Allegheny Co.
Lieutenant Colonel—Isaac Wright, of Allegheny Co.

Union Infantry,	Captain	Isaac Wright.
Sumner Infantry,	"	E. J. Seibert.
Keystone Infantry,	"	T. M. Bayne.
McClintock Guards,	"	H. W. Larimer.

* Four companies of this regiment were nine months' volunteers from Allegheny county.

ONE HUNDRED AND THIRTY-NINTH REGIMENT.

Colonel—F. H. Collier.
Lieutenant Colonel—John D. Owens.
Major—William H. Moody.
Adjutant—A. M. Harper.

Semple Infantry, A.,	Captain	Joseph R. Oxley.
" " B.,	"	Robert Munroe.
" " C,,	"	E. M. Jenkins.
" " D.,	"	James M'Gregor.
Graham Rifles,	"	J. M. Sample.
Rudd Infantry,	"	John Donald.
Logan Guards,	"	G. W. Marsh.
Armstrong Guards*	"	J. L. M'Kean.
Dudley Infantry,*	"	J. G. Parr.
Mercer Guards,†	"	A. H. Snyder.

* From Armstrong county. † From Mercer county.

ONE HUNDRED AND FIFTY-FIFTH REGIMENT.

Colonel—Edward Jay Allen.
Lieutenant Colonel—James Collard.
Major—J. H. Cain.

Hilands Guards,	Captain	A. L. Pierson.
Howard Rifles,	"	B. B. Kerr.
Kier Rifles, A.,	"	J. Collard.
Kier Rifles, B.,	"	F. Van Gorder.

Park Zouaves,	Lieut.	S. A. M'Kee.
Park Engineers,	Captain	J. H. Cain.
M'Auley Guards,	"	J. J. Hall.
Clarion Rifles,*	"	John Ewing.
Clarion Guards,*	"	—— Klotz.

* Clarion Co.

The 123d regiment left for Harrisburg on the 20th day of August, and was followed on the succeeding day by the companies subsequently organed into the 136th. The 139th left September 1st, and some days after, the 155th followed it. During this period two heavy artillery companies, the Pittsburgh Artillery, Capt. Young, and Staunton Artillery, Capt. George W. Henderson, were recruited and left for Fort Delaware, Delaware river. A battalion for the Anderson troop was recruited and forwarded to Carlisle, in this month, by Sergeant, now Major Frank B. Ward. Detachments were also recruited for Hampton's, Knap's, Daum's and other battalions in the field. These regiments had been but a few days in the field when the rebel raid into Maryland took place, threatening the safety of the Pennsylvania border. Fifty thousand militia were instantly called out by the Governor, and in less than a week a far larger number had assembled at Harrisburg. An immense war meeting was held at the Court House on September 6th, and measures were adopted for a rapid organization of the militia. Companies were hastily organized in Allegheny county, and on September 16th, 1066 men, principally from Allegheny, left for Harrisburg. A regiment had been organized, of which Robert Galway was Colonel, James M. Cooper, Lieutenant Colonel, and A. H. Gross, Major. Companies continued to rush Eastward during the ensuing week, from all the Western counties, until nearly two regiments had left Allegheny county alone. Fortunately their services were not required, and after a rapid march toward the State Line and return to Harrisburg, the companies were dismissed. They will assist, however, in maintaining an organization.

Permission having been given by the War Department to recruit a cavalry regiment, and a regiment of Infantry in Allegheny county, the "Corcoran Regiment" was set on foot, as announced, for service under General Corcoran. It proved unsuccessful, however, and the men recruited were subsequently added to other organizations, a company under Capt. Powers joining the 101st regiment, Colonel Morris. The Stanton Cavalry, Col. Schoonmaker, is still at Camp Howe, (formed for troops under the Third Requisition, at Linden Grove.) The men have been equipped, and will soon be ready to march. A regiment under Colonel Stockton is also filling rapidly.

On the 1st of August, the long anticipated order for a draft was published. The State authorities had already called upon the County Commissioners for a statement of the number of militia in the county subject to draft, but on this subject no accurate record had been kept, and in reply, the commissioners forwarded a statement compiled from the report of the County Assessors, giving the number of persons liable to military duty in the county as 12,359. Subsequently the commissioners determined to order a regular enrolment of the County, which was accordingly made. There was much discussion as to the regulations which should govern the enrolment, but we believe the state laws were followed by the assessors, who returned the number of militia liable to duty.

At its session of 1861-62, Congress passed an act authorizing the President to order a draft of the militia of the States for nine months service, fixing the limit of age between 18 and 21 years, and empowering the President, in case any State should not have the proper laws for putting the act in force, to issue regulations for a draft in such States. Under the State law, the exempts were persons in the army and navy, ministers, professors and school directors, judges, persons discharged from the U. S. service, and officers honorably discharged from militia service. The President of the United States is also exempt, and all Government officers, Custom House and Post Office officers, stage drivers and ferrymen on post routes; all Inspectors of Customs; all pilots; all sailors actually employed in the service of any citizen or merchant of the United States; with such others as are exempt by disability or chronic diseases. To secure accuracy in the enrolment, an act was passed imposing heavy penalties on all tavern or boarding house keepers or others refusing information to the Assessor, and for giving false information respecting themselves or the parties liable to enrolment.

On the 9th of August the President issued his instructions for the draft, as directed by act of Congress. These instructions provided for places of rendezvous for drafted men, and the enrolment of ALL able-bodied citizens between the ages of eighteen and forty-five. A commissioner was to be appointed for each county, and his duties prescribed as follows:

"The enrolling officers shall immediately, upon the filing of the enrolment lists, notify said Commissioners that said lists have been so filed, and the Commissioners shall thereupon give notice by handbills posted in each township of his county, of the time and place at which claims of exemption will be received and determined by him, and shall fix the time to be specified in the order aforesaid, within ten days of the filling of the enrolment from which the draft shall be made, and all persons claiming to be exempt from military duty, shall, before the said days fixed for the draft, make proof of such exemption before said Commissioner, and if found sufficient, his name shall be stricken from the list by a red line drawn through it, leaving it still legible. The Commissioner shall, in like manner strike from the list the names of all persons now in the military service of the United States—all telegraph operators and contractors actually engaged on the 5th day of August, 1862, engineers of locomotives on railroads, the Vice President of the United States, the officers, judicial and executive, of the Government of the United States, the members of the Houses of Congress and their respective officers. All custom house officers and their clerks; all Postofficers and stage drivers who are employed in the care and conveyance of the mails of the post offices of the United States; all ferrymen who are employed at any ferry on the post roads; all pilots; all mariners actually employed in the sea service of any citizens or merchants within the United States; all engineers and pilots of registered or licensed steamboats and steamships, and all persons exempt by the laws of the respective States, from military duty, on sufficient evidence, or his personal knowledge that said persons belong to any of the aforesaid classes, whether the exemption is claimed by them or not. Exemption will not be made for disability unless it be of such prominent character as to render the person unfit for service for a period of more than thirty days, to be certified by a surgeon appointed by the Governor in each county for that purpose."

Under these instructions a second enrolment of the County was made. James L. Graham, Esq., was appointed Draft Commissioner, but declined the position, and at his suggestion, the appointment was transferred to Wm. B. Negley, Esq. The Deputy Marshals appointed were the Assessors of the several precincts, who were supposed to be eminently qualified for the duty—a mistake, as it afterward proved that one man could not perform thoroughly a duty so onerous—and the enrolment proceeded rapidly. On the 20th it was announced that the total enrolment of the county was 37,099, divided as follows:

Pittsburg 11,187 | Allegheny 5,709 | Boroughs 6,870 | Townships 13,333.

The apportionment was thus announced:

	Pittsburg.	Allegheny.	Boroughs.	Townships.
Quota,	3,277	1,609	1,941	3,766
Credit,	2,016	1,354	1,752	3,236
Deficiency,	1,261	255	189	530

The total number of men reported as having enlisted in Pennsylvania organizations was 8,392, to be taken from a quota of 10,593 leaving a deficiency of 2,201. Five hundred and fifty-eight were reported as having enlisted in regiments not belonging to the State, and were therefore not credited on the quota.

The appointment of a Draft Commissioner was followed by the appointment of a Surgeon, Dr. A. C. Murdoch, to examine applicants for exemption on the ground of physical inability to bear arms. A room was assigned him in the Court House, and for several weeks his labors were most arduous. Private examinations were made in Dr. Murdoch's office, both before and after his office hours at the Court House, frequently protracting his labors far into the night. For the examinations in his private office fees were charged, giving rise to a great deal of dissatisfaction in the community, and suspicions of unfair dealing. None of the rumors were substantiated by direct charges or a legal investigation.

The labor of preparing for the draft, making the necessary calculations, etc., was so heavy that the clerks in the Draft Commissioner's office were kept busy night and day. The date fixed for drafting was twice postponed, once to Sept. 1st, and again to Thursday, Oct. 16th, the Governor, on the last occasion, announcing that the delay was occasioned by the difficulty of properly deciding the claims for exemption presented by Philadelphia and other cities. In Allegheny county great dissatisfaction was expressed in many districts at the defective returns of the Deputy Marshals, and permission was given to amend these returns up to Sept. 1st. After that date, the Commissioner refused to receive any additional returns, save those of "new enlistments"—i. e. those enlisted subsequent to the returns of the Marshals.

These additions required the certificate of the mustering officer that the parties were actually mustered into service.

A meeting held in the Third Ward subsequent to the date fixed by the Commissioner resulted in a return from the ward, by "block committees," of some three hundred names, in addition to those reported by the Deputies. These names the Commissioner declined receiving and the matter was referred to the Governor, who placed the decision entirely at the discretion of the Commissioner. Mr. Negley accordingly revised the returns, and accepted 132 names. In other wards, a large number of enlistments were found to have escaped the Deputy Marshals, but it did not become necessary to present them. The deficiency reported from the first returns of the Marshals was gradually reduced by the amended returns, until, on Monday, October 13th, the announcement was made that no draft would be required in Allegheny county.

The Pittsburg Subsistence Committee.

This noble organization owed its existence to the wants of soldiers coming into and passing through our city. When the lamented Col. Samuel W. Black was raising his regiment, several companies from the surrounding counties arrived here, and were quartered at various houses of entertainment. It was expensive, and as there was no camp opened in the vicinity, and no public provision made for subsisting the men, it was necessary that some one should become responsible for their expenses.

James Park, j r., coming to the knowledge of this state of affairs, with the liberality that has distinguished him, at once gave directions, that until further orders he "would become responsible." Mr. Park, in connection with Hon. Thomas M. Howe, then proceeded to raise a fund and to devise means to feed volunteers substantially and at a less cost than could be done at the hotels.

A meeting was held at City Hall and the following Committee appointed :—Hon. Thomas M. Howe, Chairman, B. F. Jones, Esq., George Weyman, Esq., Wm. Thaw, Esq , and John Scott, Esq.

The duty of the Committee was to attend to the subsisting of such companies as were forming, until they were regularly mustered into the U. S. service. After subsisting Col. Black's Regiment for some ten days, until they left for Washington City, the attention of the Committee was directed to the wants of the regiments and companies passing through our city. On the 28th of July, 1861, the first Regiment, the 24th Ohio, was fed by the Committee. This Regiment was ordered to report at Washington city, and passed through our city Saturday evening, July 27th. They had gone but a few miles when they were ordered back to Western Virginia. They were quartered Saturday night at City Hall, and on Sunday morning a breakfast was given to them by the Committee. As no rooms had been as yet fitted up, the meal was given to them standing in the street. The following week, the Committee had the " Old Leech Warehouse," corner of Penn and Wayne streets, fixed with tables, &c., for accommodating a regiment at one time. On Sunday morning, August 3d, 1861, the first regiment, the 20th Indiana, Col. Brown, was furnished with a substantial meal of bread and butter, ham and coffee. A number of young ladies and gentlemen was appointed by the committee to take charge of this part of the work—the giving of a meal to regiments and companies on their way to the seat of war, and on the 17th of August, 1861, the Committee resigned into the hands of these ladies and gentlemen the whole management of its operations. The following ladies and gentlemen were appointed and are still acting in that capacity, under the name of the Pittsburg Subsistence Committee.

EXECUTIVE COMMITTEE—Wm. P. Weyman, Joseph Albree, Henry M. Atwood.

ACTIVE MEMBERS.

R. C. Albree, A. H. Lane, B. F. Vandevort, B. F. Weyman, Frank Semple, George Little, O. Lemon, H. Robinson, W. B. Edwards, J. McQ. Woods, E. Schwartz, W. Young, Edward H. Nevin, Chas. Caldwell, Thos. Carnagie, Geo. W. McClure.

Misses A. Thaw, M. Morehead, E. P. Albree, J. B. Haynes, H. K. Weyman, K. Dennison, S. Townsend, E. Kennedy, A. Kennedy, M. Bryan, L. Thaw, E. P. Lane, Mrs. M. Albree, H. Moorhead, M. Bruchlocker, R. Howard, M. Howard, M. Robinson, M. Park, E. Atwood, S. Lemon, Mary Maitland, S. Breed.

Early in October, the City Councils granted the use of City Hall to the Committee, and on the 16th of October, the first regiment was fed in City Hall. The Committee has, since its organization, furnished meals to over 76,000 soldiers. Of this number, 5768 were sick and wounded. These were provided with medical attendance, and all comforts their situation demanded.

The Committee, after receiving several appeals for supplies from some of the Hospitals of our Army, on the 15th of January, 1862, opened depots for receiving donations of Hospital Supplies. They have forwarded, up to Oct. 1st, 320 large cases of supplies to the different Hospitals East and West, containing 54,946 articles. Amongst the articles there were 4800 shirts, 2140 drawers, 2025 pillows, 1450 cans fruit, and other articles in proportion. The ladies of the Committee under the management of Miss A. Thaw, meet every Wednesday afternoon, at City Hall, where they cut out work and give it to any persons willing to make it up. In this way over 2,000 shirts and pairs of drawers have been made during the past six months. The Committee depends altogether on voluntary contributions for its support.

Amount of contributions of cash for Feeding Fund,		$5,500
" " Provisions,		500
		$6,000
Amount of contributions of cash and articles for Hospitals,		$31,250

We can only say, in conclusion, that Committee has performed its work well and thoroughly, yet without public demonstration. They have earned the warm gratitude of thousands of way-worn soldiers, who, without their kind assistance, would have gone on their journey uncheered and unrefreshed. Verily, they have earned their reward.

The number of pages of religious Books and papers distributed at the rooms of the Committee amongst soldiers passing through our city was 246,000.

THE BOUNTY FUND SUBSCRIPTION.

We publish below a classified list of the sums subscribed to the fund for paying a bounty of fifty dollars to volunteers from Allegheny county. The list includes all subscriptions above $50, our space forbidding the publication of smaller sums. In some cases the amounts returned from wards include sums above fifty, and where these could be obtained they have been included in the classified list.

$5,000.

Pittsburg Bank,
Exchange Bank,

$3,000.

Merchants & Manufac. Bank,
Citizens' Bank,

$2500.

Allegheny Bank,

$2,000.

Knapp, Rudd & Co.,
Clarke & Thaw,

$1500.

Iron City Bank,
Mechanics Bank,
P., Ft. Wayne & Chicago RR.,

$1,000.

Farmers' Deposit Bank,
Pittsburg Trust Co,.
Dollar Savings Bank,
James Park, jr.,
Thomas M. Howe,

Wm. Bagaley,
A. & W. Nimick,
Singer, Nimick & Co.,
All'y. Suspension Bridge,
G. &. J. H. Shoenberger,
Zug & Painter,
Isaac Jones,
Western Insurance Co.,
Graff, Bennett & Co.,
Bollman & Garrison,
Pittsburg Gas Co.,
Mrs. Harmar Denny.

$750.

Adams Express Co.,

$500.

J. K. Moorhead,
White, Orr & Co.,
Jones & Laughlin,
Knapp, Wood & Co.,
John Bissell,
Eliza Shields,
Hanna, Hart & Co.,
Hays & Stewart,
M'Cord & Co.,
M'Candless, Jamison & Co.,
Jno. Dunlap & Co.,

John I. House & Co.,
Wilson, M'Elroy & Co.,
S. Jones & Co.,
Wilson, Carr & Co.,
Everson, Preston & Co.,
Hailman, Rahm & Co.,
Lloyd & Black,
N. Holmes & Sons,
Wm. M'Cully & Co.,
Lewis, Dalzell & Co.,
Monongahela Navigation Co.,
Watt & Co.,
Moorhead & Co.,
James H. Hays,
R. Patrick & Co.,
H. Childs & Co.,
Thos. A. Scott,
R. H. Hartley & Co.,
James Wood & Co.,
John B. Semple,
B. A. Fahnestock,
James B. Lyon,
A. & D. H. Chambers,
Arbuthnot & Shannon,
John Dean,
Robinson, Minis & Millers,
Monongahela Bridge Co.,
R. T. Kennedy & Bro.,

Thos. Bakewell,
Livingston, Copeland & Co.,
Spang, Chalfant & Co.,
Kramer & Rahm,
Geo. W. Jackson,
King, Pennock & Co.,
J. M'Cully & Co.,
Miller & Ricketson,
George W. Cass,
Hostetter & Smith,
Andrew Fulton,
John Floyd,
S. S. Fowler & Co.,
J. P. Hanna & Co.,
Dilworth, Porter & Co.,
James L. Graham,
James Marshall,
Union Banking Co.,
Citizens Insurance Co.,
Monongahela Insurance Co.,
Eureka Insurance Co.,
German T. & S. Bank,

$375.

James M. Cooper.

$300.

Birm. & Pitts. Bridge Co.,
John P. Pears,
Weyman & Son,
S. Riddle & Co.,
T. H. Nevin & Co.,
Pittsburg Insurance Co.,
Bryce, Richards & Co.,

$250.

Wm. M. Shinn,
Thompson Bell & Co.,
Penna. Salt Manuf. Co.,
Lippencott & Co.,
Thomas Wightman,
R. S. Hays,
James Dalzell & Son,
W. & H. Walker,
Chess, Smith & Co.,
Charles M'Knight,
Delaware Mutual Ins. Co.,
Pennsylvania Ins. Co.

$200.

Aladdin Oil Co.,
Logan & Gregg,
W. H. Lowrie,
John Harper,
Neville B. Craig,
A. M. Wallingford,
T. & J. T. M'Cance,
Joseph Horne,
F. Sellers & Co.,
William Wilkins,
Postley, Nelson & Co.,
Whitmore, Wolf, Duff & Co.,
Means & Coffin,

Anderson & Phillips,
Mair & Davidson,
William Morrison,
William Semple,
James A. Hutchison,
Hon. William Wilkins,
W. E. Schmertz & Co.,
Mitchell, Herron & Co.,

$150.

Maffitt & Old,
Pennock, Hart & Co.,
D. Fitzsimmons & Sons,
George Albree.

$125.

Forsyth Bro. & Co.,

$100.

A. Bradley,
Robert Lea,
H. B. Wilkins,
William Dilworth, jr.,
J. L. Marshall,
S. Blackmore & Co.,
Samuel M'Kee, (9th ward)
M'Donald & Arbuckle,
J. K. Wilson,
R. D. Cochran,
Henry W. Oliver,
E. H. Irish,
D. R. Galway,
S. Harbaugh & Co.,
R. L. M'Grew,
Joshua Rhodes,
John A. Renshaw,
C. A. Dravo,
A. H. Harvey & Co.,
Mrs. Ann Beard,
William S. Haven,
Bissell & Co.,
Olnhausen, Crawford & Co.,
Rev. E. McMahon,
John A. Caughey,
Robert Beer,
John Graham,
William B. Haslett,
C. L. Brennan,
John S. McMillen,
W. & D. Rinehart,
Reymer Brothers,
Neeb, Bauer & Co.,
E. Simpson,
James S. Craft,
A. H. English & Co.,
R. C. Loomis,
Head & Metzgar,
Robert Dalzell,
Alex. H. Miller,
Wm. McClintock & Son,
G. W. Coffin,
Wood & Lukens,
Samuel Gormley,

W. W. Martin,
John W. Spencer,
Preston & Porter,
George P. Hamilton,
Thomas D. Messler,
Kelly, Glass & Co.,
Jos. Woodwell & Co.,
J. L. Carnahan,
Wm. H. Smith & Co.,
John B. Jones,
James W. Woodwell,
Lucesco Oil Co.,
Altenburg, Reddick & Co.,
Ardesco Oil Co.,
Wm. G. Johnston & Co.,
J. F. Hamilton & Co.,
Fitzsimmons & Morrow,
Reuben Miller, jr.,
Wilson & Gorman,
Samuel M. Lane,
C. C. Boyd,
Hill, M'Clurg & Co.,
Morganstern & Bro.,
Duncan, Dunlap & Co.,
Dr. J. A. Reed,
J. & H. Phillips,
A. Holstein,
Shumaker & Lang,
F. Bausman,
North American Oil Co.,
John Arthurs,
Fleming Brothers,
John McDevitt,
A. Frowenfield & Bro.,
Alexander Speer,
E. Edmondson & Co.,
Robert Finney,
T. B. Young & Co.,
Kean & Keller,
Andrew Ackley,
Jared M. Brush,
James Rees,
J. S. Liggett & Co.,
Caldwell & Bro.,
S. Severance,
Hartupee & Co.,
Long & Duff,
George A. Berry & Co.,
Wm. Mackeown,
C. W. Batchelor,
Charles J. Clark,
Elias D. Kennedy,
Andrew D. Smith,
Wm. M. Faber & Co.,
Kay & Co.,
Henry Collins,
Alexander Gordon,
D. Z. Brickel,
Wm. Pickersgill,
Nicholas Voeghtly,
R. F. Leech,
Geo. B. Jones,
B. P. Bakewell,

J. P. Haigh,
Foster & Fleeson,
James P. Barr,
R. H. Palmer,
J. M. Snowden & Co.,
Wm. Cooper & Co.,
Graham & Thomas,
J. W. Barker & Co.,
W. Bryant & Co.,
J. Laughrey & Co.,
A. McFarland,
Thomas Moore,
Wm. M. Gormley,
Watson & Armstrong,
Wm. Harbaugh,
J. H. Jones,
John H. Mellor,
J. McD. Crossan,
Marshall & Bro.,
H. Woods,
W. S. Bissell,
Tiernan & Getty,
J. D. Baldwin,
J. Voeghtly & Co.,
H. Sproul,
A. Cameron,
R. H. Davis,
Robert McKnight,
A. M Marshall & Co.,
C. Yeager,
Thompson & Groetzinger,
H. P. Schwartz,
D. L. Shields,
Forrester & Megraw,
John Nevin, jr.,
W. B. Pusey,
G. E. Warner,
Henry Palmer,
Alex Miller, (Ohio tp.)
Thos. Mellon,
John Scott,
R. C. Grier Sproul,
A. Bates,
Joseph H. Hill,
George R. White,
John Roup,
John Liggett,
J. & D. E. Bayard,
Hays & Getty,
Fleming & Torrens,
Watson & Monroe,

Davage & Roberts,
Richey & Finkbine,
James Thorn & Co.,
C. Burchfield,
Samuel Cooper,
John Orr & Co.,
John Irwin,
M'Quewan & Douglass.
Carroll & Snyder,
John R. M Cune,
H. Kleber & Co.,
Lambert & Shipton,
White Brothers,
D. Gregg & Co.,
W. & D. Hugus
Robinson & Co.,
B. C. & J. H. Sawyer,
John Sampson,
J. & D. Frazier,
Phelps, Park & Co.,
Fred. M'Kee,
Ch. Ihsen,
Thomas M'Kee,
John P. Pears,
James M'Kee,
Christian Siebert,
Samuel H. Keller,
Joseph Patterson,

$75

J P. Henderson,
Jos. Meyers & Bro's.,

$50

James P. Sterrett,
J. H. Demler,
John H. Oliver,
W. H. Whitacre,
A Guckheimer & Brs.,
J. Brooks,
Samuel Bradley,
J. R. Weldin,
N. J. Smith,
W. T. Purviance,
George Shiras.
L. P. Hitchcock,
Cornwall & Kerr,
George H. Anderson,
S. F. Von Bonhorst,
John Ogden & Co.,
J. J. Siebeneck,

J. A. Mazurie,
B. F. Collins,
T. A. Evans & Co.,
F. M. Gordon,
Thos. Graff,
Samuel Wilson,
Wm. M. Roberts,
J. M. Tiernan,
Grobe & Moretz,
Jacob Hoffman, Gov't Contractor, not paid.
Jas. Caldwell,
A. Hobson,
Samuel Gordon,
W. D. Riddle,
Thos. Arnold,
P. H. Kauffman,
Mrs. Wm. Semple,
Geo. G. Negley,
Wm. S. Brown,
Douglass & English,
Guthrie & Sill,
William Rea,
J. H. Jenkins,
J. B. Hubley,
Haworth & Bros.,
W. Haslage & Co.,
J. Henderson & Bro.,
John P. Scott,
James Gardiner,
Hammer & Dauler,
Nicholas Needer,
J. H. Robinson,
J. A. Kaercher,
Mrs. L. M. D. Detheridge,
Jacob Booberger,
Edw. Ditheridge,
A. Clendenning,
Wm. M. Hersh,
Henry Whitfield,
Conway & M'Gowan,
Edward Wilkins,
Z. Wainright,
R. L. Ewalt,
David Holmes,
James Irwin,
Smith & Earle,
Joseph Schmidt,
Pastor of St. Philomina's
    Church,

Lawrenceville,	-	-	- $1,055 00	Tarentum Borough,	-	- 384 00
3d Ward, Pittsburg,	-	- 4,531 00	Birmingham do,	-	- - 969 00
4th Ward, Allegheny,	-	- 1,102 00	Patton Township,	-	- - 127 00
1st Ward, Pittsburg,	-	- 7,504 00	Crescent do.,	-	- - 131 25
5th Ward, do,	-	- 1,073 25	Findlay do.,	-	- - 479 00
4th Ward, do,	-	- 3,802 00	Duquesne Borough,	-	- 368 00
2nd Ward, do,	-	- 6,330 00	Reserve Township,	-	- 555 00
8th Ward, do,	-	- 618 00	Upper St. Clair do.,	-	- 90 00
3d Ward, Allegheny,	-	- 1,371 50	Manchester Borough,	-	- 680 00
6th Ward, Pittsburg,	-	- 615 60	M'Candless Township,	-	- 78 00
Peebles & Collins Tps.,	-	1,763 50	Mechanics Bank, Allegheny,	-	2,850 00

Subscription to Loans.

For still further proof of the loyalty of Allegheny county to the Union, we give the amounts subscribed by her citizens to the different loans, National and State:

To the 7-30 Government loan, three hundred and twenty-seven subscriptions were made, amounting in the aggregate to $520,404 89, from Sept. 16th to Dec. 2d, 1861, at which time the books were closed.

To the Six per cent. Government loan $532,432 was subscribed from May 21st to Oct. 14, 1862. We could not obtain the number of the subscribers, a convenient record not being obtainable.

These subscriptions were made at the office of Joshua Hanna, Esq., of Hanna, Hart & Co., Bankers, corner of Third and Wood streets. At least $500,000 additional was taken in the east by parties resident in the county.

Of the $3,000,000 State loan, authorized by an act of the Legislature, approved May 15, 1862, the following amounts were taken by Banks of this city:

Bank of Pittsburg, $90,000; Exchange Bank, $90,000; Merchants & Manufacturers' Bank, $50,000; Citizens Bank, $50,000; Iron City Bank, $40,000; Allegheny Bank, $40,000; Mechanics Bank, $30,000. Total, $390,000.

The aggregate amount taken of the loans by citizens and corporations of Allegheny county, (including the half million taken in the east,) is $1,942,283 89.

Subscriptions to the six per cent. loan are still being made, our report of the amount taken, as given above, being up to the 14th of October last.

Uniforming the Three Months Men.

No provision having been made, either in this city or in Harrisburg, by the authorities, in 1861, for uniforming the three months volunteers, the men demurred from going until they were suitably clothed. B. F. Jones, Esq., assumed the task of equipping one company, and depositing his check for three thousand dollars, ordered the clothing to be furnished, and set about collecting the amount to reimburse himself. With what success his labors were crowned will be shown below. Over thirteen thousand dollars were collected in a day or two, and with this ten companies were uniformed.

Beside these, several other companies were supplied with uniforms, by private subscription, of which, however, we can find no record.

This sum was subscribed with the understanding that it should be refunded by the State, and the larger part of the donors have agreed, in case it should be thus returned, that it should be appropriated for the relief of distressed families of volunteers. As yet, the State has done nothing either in this case, or in that of Messrs. Morganstern & Bro. who furnished one entire company, for which they have never received one cent. The members of the Legislature for this county should see that this just claim against the Commonwealth be not allowed to slumber during the approaching session. The amount subscribed for the clothing will undoubtedly inure to the benefit of some one of our War charities.

In some cases uniforms for commissioned officers were furnished out of this fund, a fact that should be stated in justice to the contractors, as otherwise the disparity between the prices charged per suit would attract attention.

$300	Kean & Keller,	Lyon, Shorb & Co.,
Bank of Pittsburgh,	Spang, Chalfant & Co.,	Zug & Painter,
200	Lloyd & Black.	Wm. Bagaley,
Thomas Wightman,	Everson, Preston & Co.,	James Laughlin,
100	Singer, Nimick & Co.,	M'Knight & Bro.,
B. F. Jones,	Nimick & Co.,	B. A. Fahnestock & Co.
M. K. Moorhead,	Graff, Bennett & Co.,	John Holmes,
Joseph Plumer,	James A. Hutchison,	Hailman, Rahm & Co.,
James Herdman,	Chess, Smyth & Co.,	James Dalzell & Son,
Joseph Dilworth,	James Wood & Co.,	A. Fulton,
Francis Sellers,	A. & D. H. Chambers,	Fleming Bros.,
A. Bradley,	Wm. M'Cully & Co.,	Thos. L. Shields,
John Bissell,	Bakewell, Pears & Co.,	Penn'a. Salt Manufacturing Co.
C. W. Ricketson,	Park, M'Curdy & Co.,	S. H. Keller,
Semple & Jones,	John I. House & Co.,	Arbuthnot & Shannon,
Clarke & Co.,	Livingston, Copeland & Co.,	John Scott,
	Phillips & Best,	B. L. Fahnescok & Co.,
	Isaac Jones,	John Anderson & Son,

Wm. J. Morrison,
Jones, Wallingford & Co.,
S. H. Hartman,
Bailey, Brown & Co.,
S. M. Kier,
Wm. Carr,
Wm. B. Hays & Co.,
John McDevitt,
Watt & Wilson,
Jacob Painter & Co.,
Jas. McCully & Co.,
John Floyd & Co.,
J. & J. W. Woodwell,
Wm. M. Gormley & Co.,
Robert Dalzel & Co.,
Felix R. Brunot,
Head & Metzgar,
Bissell & Co.,
James O'Hara,
H. Childs & Co.,
McCord & Co.,
Mair & Davidson,
J. C. Bidwell,
Wilson, Carr & Co.,
Bryce, Richards & Co.,
James O'Connor,
Hanna, Hart & Co.,
Wilson, McElroy & Co.,
S. Jones & Co.,
D. Gregg & Co.,
W. Bryant,
R. H. Hartley & Co.,
Rhodes & Verner,
Charles H. Paulson,
Kramer & Rahm,
Thomas M. Howe,
McClurkan, Herron & Co.,

Lewis, Dalzell & Co.,
G. & J. H. Shoenberger,
Alexander King,
James B. Lyon & Co.,
M'Candless, Jamison & Co.,
Fitzsimmons & Morrow,
O. Blackburn,
T. & J. T. McCance,
William Cooper & Co.,
J. M. Little,
James C. Watt,
C. Yeager & Co.,
W. McClintock,
Mitchell, Herron & Co.,
Brown & Kirkpatricks,
Lambert & Shipton,
McDonald & Arbuckles,
J. R. M'Cune,
Lucisco Oil Co.,
Bollman & Garrison,
Morganstern & Bro.,
C. Ihmsen & Sons,
N. Holmes & Sons,
George W. Jackson,
James M'Auley,
S. M'Kee & Co.,
A. Frowenfield & Bro.,
Shriver & Dilworth
Lavely, Park & Co.,

50.

W. W. Martin,
Long & Duff,
John Moorhead,
Caldwell & Bro.,
James H. Hays,
J. S. Liggett,

James Holmes & Co.,
S. Dilworth & Co.,
Lippincott & Co.,
Cunningham & Co.,
Newmyer, Graff & Co.,
Richard Hays,
Harbaugh & Co.,
Hitchcock, M'Creery & Co.,
Daniel Wallace,
Samuel M'Crickart & Co.,
John Parker,
Knox & Parker,
Francis G. Bailey,
R. Robinson & Co.,
Geo. R. White,
A. Speer,
Geo. A. Berry & Co.,
Reymer & Brothers,
Shacklett, M'Lain & Co.,
Wm. Dilworth, jr.,
John A. Renshaw,
M. De Lange,
J. J. Gillespie,
Beck & Lazear,
J. Henderson & Bro.,
S. George & Co.
E. H. Myers & Co.,

25

Wm. H. Smith & Co.,
James Boyd,
Means & Coffin,
M'Whinney, Hare & Co.,
B. Wolff, jr.,
Wm. M'Cutcheon,

Disbursed as Follows :

DUQUESNE GREYS, Co. A., Capt. David Campbell,

Paid Morganstern & Bro., for 85 uniforms, under garments, overcoats and blankets, - - - - - - $2,523 70

DUQUESNE GREYS, Co. B., Capt. John Poland,

Paid Morganstern & Bro., for 82 uniforms, - - - - - 1,130 00

UNION CADETS, Capt. John W. Patterson,

Paid Louis Kiehneison, for 82 uniforms, - - - - $720 00
" 84 caps, - - - - - 84 00— 804 00

WASHINGTON INFANTRY, Capt. T. A. Rowley, Comp'ys A, B, C,

Paid J. M. Little, for 250 uniforms, - - - - - - 3,960 00

JACKSON INDEPENDENT BLUES, Capt. S. M'Kee,

Paid Morganstern & Bro., for 82 uniforms, - - - - - 1,055 50

ZOUAVE CADETS,

Paid J. C. Watt, for 92 uniforms, - - - - - - 1,104 00

FIREMEN'S LEGION, Capt. John H. Stewart,

Paid A. Frowenfield & Bro., for 90 uniforms, - - - - 1,228 00

IRON CITY GUARDS, Capt. W. M. Gormley,

Paid J. C. Watt, for 77 uniforms, - - - - - 1,162 50
84 caps, - - - - - 92 40— 1,254 90

PITTSBURGH INVINCIBLES, Capt. Wm. Trovillo,

Paid for Recruiting Expenses,	142 20

SHIELDS GUARDS, Capt. W. C. Gallagher,

Paid for Recruiting Expenses,	100 00

SCOTT LEGION, Capt. O. H. Rippey,

Paid for Recruiting Expenses,	100 00
Paid C. H. Paulson, for 360 caps,	279 20

$13,681 50

IN CONCLUSION.

Any attempt to condense the record of the last eighteen months—a period so full of important events—into the brief limits of a pamphlet, must necessarily be imperfect. The labor of collecting the facts presented in the foregoing pages would not be credited by any one not familiar with the confused state of affairs which marked the periods of recruiting following each call for troops. *There exists in Allegheny county no official or reliable record of the troops which have left it,* and the columns of the daily newspapers—accessible to but few and necessarily inaccurate—furnish the only data in relation to the regiments of gallant men now in service. The errors and omissions in our record must be attributed to this fact.

At the conclusion of the Draft Commissioner's labors it was shown that twelve thousand six hundred and ninety men were in Pennsylvania service from Allegheny county, and we have no doubt that the members in service in organizations not belonging to the State, will increase this number to fifteen thousand men. The Committee has paid $50 bounty to 1664 men, and $10 bounty, with county bond for $50, to 2326 men. Total 3990.

The liberality of the people of Allegheny county has been displayed, since the outbreak of the rebellion, by contributions of money and other necessary articles for the outfit of troops, care of sick and wounded soldiers, supplying traveling regiments, supporting families of absent men, and contributing to the support of the government by loans of money. Our record shows the collection of the following amounts:

Of 7:30 and 6 per cent. loans taken in the county	$1,942,283,89
For volunteer's bounty fund, under Executive Committee	129,225,05
Voluntary Subscriptions to Relief Fund	24,251,90
Subsistence Committee in food and Hospital supplies	27,250,00
Subscription to private fund for uniforms	13,681,50

Total	2,136,692,34

This sum, it will be remembered, does not include the sums given by individuals to companies, nor the hundreds of private benefactions of every description, which probably have not been less than one hundred thousand.

In closing our sketch of the events transpiring in and around our city, in relation to the rebellion, we deem it but a fitting tribute to those worthy gentlemen, who have served their country and the cause so efficiently, to say that by the active and unremitting spirit of comparatively a few of our citizens, was the abundant patriotism of Allegheny County given shape and direction. To Hon. Thomas M. Howe, James Parke, Jr., John Harper, Hon. Wm. Wilkins, Thomas Bakewell, Reuben Miller, Jr., Isaac Jones, James M'Auley, F. R. Brunot, Wm. F. Johnston, Geo. W. Cass, W. M. Shinn, James A. Hutchison, and some others equally deserving, do we owe the origination, and the successful development, of the greater part of the plans which have resulted in placing in the field nearly 14,000 soldiers from Allegheny County, and for placing their families, at least, beyond the reach of want.

And without desiring to seem invidious, we may say that no two soldiers in the field have rendered their country greater service than Hon. T. M. Howe and James Parke, Jr., have done in the business departments of war matters at home. Possessed of business ability in an unsurpassable degree, above suspicion for sinister motives in the way of seeking or controlling business patronage, Mr. Howe has at all times been found ready and willing to sacrifice every domestic comfort, every private consideration, for the public good. At present he is the A. A. General for Western Pennsylvania, a position which could certainly confer no honor upon the worthy ex-Representative of this great manufacturing district, and which he was only induced to accept at the earnest solicitation of the Executive. His services have indeed been arduous, and that they have been productive of good fruit, the honorable exemption of Allegheny County from the operations of the draft is a living proof.

Of Mr. Parke's services, little less can be said. As in the case of Mr. Howe, his purse strings were always open, and however distasteful it may be to these really unobtrusive, yet public spirited gentlemen, to be thus brought to notice, we would deem ourselves derelict in our duty as faithful chroniclers, were we to pass them over.

Some ill-feeling has been created in the community by the number of persons exempt under the "disability" clause of the law. The proper course, it is now conceded, is to put ALL names in the wheel—drafting a sufficient number to cover the loss by examination—and permit all who can to make good their claims to exemption. But this was not the law, and of course the preliminary examinations ordered, had to be made. That a large proportion of volunteer recruits become inmates of military hospitals, before leaving their camps of instruction, is well known, and a worse state of affairs was to be expected among the drafted men. It should be remembered that among the volunteer force much the larger portion have been from the working classes, men who by daily manual toil generally escape functional disorders—while the drafted troops will include a considerable number of mercantile and professional men—a class subject to such disorders. It was desirable to avoid, as far as possible, the drafting of men whose liability to constitutional or functional disorders would render them unfit for service on the first exposure, and in view of these facts the Department ordered the preliminary examination. A duty so delicate as the decision on claims of physical disability, necessarily involved a liability to occasional error, and the only alternative was to decide as carefully, yet as leniently, as justice would permit. Some may have been exempted in this county who were less unfitted than others who entered no claim, but they were unquestionably forced to present the strongest proofs of their allegations. This the law requires—beyond it, the Surgeon could not go, whatever professional jealousy may have insinuated to the contrary. Those who have joined in the murmurings against Dr. Murdoch, the Examining Surgeon for this county, should bear these facts in mind, and as a simple act of justice learn the proofs on which each case was decided, before prejudging its unfairness.

Of the Sanitary Commissions of Allegheny County we had intended to speak at length, but were compelled to forego so doing, having failed to obtain any definite data. Our citizens sent commissions at various times to Eastern Virginia, (on the Peninsula) and also to the South-West, to ascertain the condition and wants of our soldiers, and fully prepared to render all aid necessary to their comfort, whether wounded, sick, or in want of clothing or the necessaries of life. Steamboats were sent to Tennessee, shortly subsequent to the battle of Shiloh, with physicians and nurses and an abundance of hospital stores, returning in due time, after having rendered very efficient aid in properly providing for invalid soldiers, transporting some 400 from the immediate scene of that sanguinary struggle. Of this expedition F. R. Brunot, Esq., had the superintendence, and most faithfully and satisfactorily discharged his trust.

ADDENDA.

On page 28th, in speaking of the National Cavalry, Capt. Boyce, we should have added that the company was attached to the 1st Penna. Cavalry, Col. Bayard, and participated in some brilliant dashes in the vicinity of Fredericksburg and on the Peninsula. Capt. Boyce resigned on account of ill-health, and 1st Lieut. Williams succeeded to the command.

Another company of Cavalry, under command of Capt. Ormsby Robinson, composed exclusively of Allegheny county men, is attached to one of the Pennsylvania regiments, and saw active service on the Peninsula, under Col. Averill. The cavalry company of Capt. Faith is in the 5th Regiment, Col. David Campbell, not in the 4th, lately commanded by Col. J. H. Childs. Capt. Patrick Kane also recruited a cavalry company, which he took east and there joined a regiment in an Irish brigade. Capt. Hays raised a company, which was attached to Col. Emory's 6th (regular) cavalry.

We have omitted to speak of Thompson's battery, composed of Allegheny county men, and recruited under the auspices of Gen. W. H. Lamon, authorized to raise a brigade, in which, however, he did not succeed, the troops temporarily under his control, being assigned to different corps.

Five steamboats were fitted out at this port, as rams, during the present year, viz: Mingo, Capt. Bausman; Lioness, Capt. Shroades; Samson, Capt. Porter; D. Fulton, Capt. Dalzell; T. D. Horner, Capt. Cadman. These boats took away 110 men as crews.

NOTE.—We have been requested by Dr. A. C. Murdoch, Examining Surgeon for Allegheny Co., to state that the name of Alexander Addison Miller, of Pitt Township, which appears among the names of those exempted upon a disability certificate, appears in that light, upon the record of Commissioner Negley, through a mistake, Mr. Miller having never applied for exemption, through any cause whatever.

LIST OF EXEMPTS.

ABBREVIATIONS.—d. c., disability certificate; o. a., over age; en. e., enrolled elsewhere; m. c., mail carrier; tel. op., telegraphic operator; p. m. postmaster; s. d., school director; p. d., poor director; dis. discharged from the army.

PITTSBURGH.

FIRST WARD.

Chas Burkhardt, al
Isaac Bierman, d c
Chas Bierman, d c
Jacob Beuswanger, d c
Owen Clark, alien
Bernard Carr, d c
Morgan Conely, o a
Arthur Clinton, d c
Richard Cass, d c
Hugh Dickson, d c
Jacob Diamond, d c
Wm V Diehl, d c
Sol J Dehaern, al
Thos Faherty, d c
Pat Fitzsimmons, d c
Wm Frank, d c
Abraham Fryer, d c
Neal Gaines, d c
Adams Getty, d c & s d
Gustave Graefner, d c
John Gete, d c
Peter Horty, o a
Mart Holran, alien
Jno Hanlon, alien
Benson P Jones, d c
Peter Jacobs, d c
Henry Krusman, o a
Wm Kohlbepp, o a
John King, d c
Edwin Kincaid, d c
Patrick Keefe, alien
Edwin Lowe, o a
John Lavely, d c
Joseph Levaler, alien
Patrick Murray, d c
Jas R Myers, d c

Timothy Maloney, d c
Dennis O'Connor, alien
Peter Pile, d c
Sam G Patterson, eng'r
John L Pichl, pensioner
George Rice, d c
John W Reynolds, dis
John E Rheams, d c
Samuel Rheams, d c
Edward Ryan, dis
Benj W Robbins, o a
Clemens Ropp, d c
Patrick Ragan, d c
Samuel Rheams, sr, dis
John Stone, d c
Andrew Sumaker, d c
Thomas Sloan, dis
John Slyder, d c
L E Smith, eng'r
George Maixell, d c
Philip Hout, d c
Westley Couthart, d c
Lawrence Cavanaugh, alien
Patrick O'Connor. d c
Leopold Cohn, d c
Simon Citran, alien
Chas P Caughey, d c
Wm D Cooper, d c
Saml P Collins, s d
Chas Ennant, d c
Robert C Elliott, d c
David L Evans, dis
Saml M Evans, d c
James Foley, o a
John Funk, d c
Patk Foley, dis

Peter Folen, dis
Peter Folcy, dis
John Gross, dis
Jas Hickey, o a
Myers Hanaur, d c
Peter Hetzler, alien
John Johnston, alien
Michl M'Donough, alien
John M'Graw, d c
Owen M'Cabe, d c
Daniel M'Gonnigle, d c
Aug M'Elachy, d c
Joines M'Arree, d c
Milton M'Clelland, d c
Wm Noble, alien
Owen O'Neill, alien
Benj Oppenheimer, d c
Wm K Oglesbee, d c
Christian Starz, alien
John F Stockdale, d c
George Shaw, alien
Frank Snyder, d c
Emil Schauberth, alien
John Shaler, d c
Valentine Sheter, d c
Edwin Strain, alien
John H Sarber, d c
Jerry Tool, alien
John Wanderly, d c
Eph Worsner, o a
Samuel Werthermer, d c
Isaac Werthermer, d c
Jacob Wells, o a
Lewis Walters, d c
Alex Walker, alien
Patrick Welsh, alien

SECOND WARD.

Addison Arthurs, d c
Biddle Arthurs, d c
J C Boyd, d c
A F Brackemeyer, d c
Moses Beatty, alien
Hugh Boyle, alien
Alex Behler, d c
Wm Barrett, d c
C C Cochran, teacher
Michl Carroll, o a
Jos G Caldwell, m c
A M Byers, d c
Henry Burch, alien
W W Burchfield, d c
Geo M Bliss, o a
Geo W Beltzhoover, o a
Con Harkins, alien
Robt P Biddle, d c
Jno Cunningham, d c
Tim Cadman, o a
Jas Dolans, d c
Josiah F Day, d c
T W Davis, d c
C M Davis, arsenal
T B Davitt, o a
Ed M Davis, arsenal
Ed Donelly, o a
Morris Eisner, d c
Leopold Eisner, d c
II Fleshman, d c
Ferd Fisher, d c
Stephen Falls, en e
Robt Fife, alien
Dan Kinzee, d c
J B Kilgore, d c
C II Kinkerly, d c
II J Lance, alien
Geo Lang, d c
Dennis Manshin, alien
Wm Means, d c
W C Murphy, d c
L Markle, pension agent
J K Morange, d c
W P Marshall, d c
B M'Minoman, d c
Felix M'Closky, d c

Jas Matthews, pilot
B M'Glaughlin, d c
Wm M'Kenna, alien
C C Mellor, d c
W S M'Dowell, d c
Jas M'Clelland, d c
David Morgan, alien
T G M'Cormack, n r
C Mensinger, d c
E B Matthews, d c
D J M'Donald, d c
L Morganstern, d c
J Morganstern, o a
C W Millard, eng C RR
Thos Moore, d c
H II Nieman, d c
J Necomer, o a
Jas Orr, d c
Daniel O'Neill, d c
James O'Neil, d c
W Owens, Jr, d c
John O'Keef, o a
Jas Phelan, d c
Andrew Goering, d c
David Gilgey, d c
A F Gabler, en e
R J Grace, o a
John Herron, d c
Leo Highbruner, d c
C Hasbrouck, s d
Lucius W Henry, d c
Henry Hartman, d c
Jacob Hershfield, d c
J A Harton, eng'r
T M Harton, d c
John Hanly, alien
Wm Harpin, d c
Pat Goghegan, d c
O Hickman, alien
D II Hazen, d c
Thos Hulings, d c
Wm H House, d c
W S Jackson, d c
Lewis Jaroslowski, d c
Wm Jenkins, alien
Jas Irwin, d c

Thos Irwin, d c
Geo Irvin, d c
P M Kirwan, alien
Michl Keenan, alien
Francis Kennedy, alien
J G Kendal, tel op
Christ Kimmer, alien
Wm Kyle, o a
W K Pierce, d c
C F Porter, d c
Wm Pinkerton, d c
S Paisley, alien
E Reineman, d c
John Roxbury, alien
Jasper E Sergeant, d c
H Samson, d c
C A Stevens, eng'r
E Slatterick, o a
II Stamm, d c
Harry Shirls, d c
Daniel Steen, d c
Solomon Stein, n r
Samuel Seeds, alien
Jos Sperry, d c
Edw Seither, d c
David Stein, o a
Wm Skillett, alien
J A Teece, alien
Albert Thomas, d c
John Torrence, d c
Patrick Tighe, alien
H Thorthurn, alien
S Williams, d c
D Woolslayer, d c
W Weyman, d c
H O Wefing, d c
Henry Wolker, alien
R S Waring, d c
J Winterburn, d c
G Ernest, dis
James M'Laughlin, alien
Kennedy Marshall, d c
John R Bangorst, p o clk
C A Von Bonhorst, p o clk
Wm Woods, poor director

THIRD WARD.

Michael Malone, d c
Jos Larkin, d c
Florence Sullivan, o a
Fred Bushman, o a
Patrick M'Carthy, alien
Thomas Hamilton, alien
Jeremiah Downey, d c
A Harland, preacher
Andrew B Hayden, d c
Christopher Hellymer, d c
Garnet Bultman, d c

Patrick M'Afee, d c
John Coffey, o a
John Hooper, alien
John Fitzgerald, o a
Timothy Kinney, d c
Hugh Duffey, d c
John Mooney, d c
Jeremiah Sullivan, d c
Alex Wells, n r
W V R Smith, d c
John Burngerst, alien

Henry A Fryvogle, d c
James Herley, alien
Wm Ryan, o a
Wm S Lavely, o a
Peter Caveney, d c
Patk Leonard, o a
Michael Lynch, alien
John Sullivan, alien
John Donavon, d c
Edward P Kearns, d c
Frederick Gross, d c

Henry Lang, d c
Peter Brown, o a
Jos G Pollock, d c
Anthony Dougherty, alien
Uriah S Bokoler, n r
Sidney G Stewart, d c
Thos C Warrington, alien
John Griffen, d c
Edward Faunell, alien
Oscar M'Millan, d c
E J Smith, d c
Lincoln Oldshue, d c
Patrick Regan, alien
Patrick Donnelly, d c
Thos Commond, o a
Patrick Flinn, d c
William Smith, d c
Thos Cowell, alien
Jas B Williams, d c
Christian Diehl, d c
Jacob F Steele, d c
Frederick Rust, d c
Stephen Barton, d c
Joseph Anchem, alien
Francis M'Grath, o a
Frederick Roenig, d c
Michael Egan, d c
Chas Gross, d c
Fredk Anderson, alien
John Dunn, alien
Thomas Day, alien
Philip Phillipson, alien
Fred Gerberding, d c
Patrick Mellon, d c
Moses Godhelp, d c
Leopold Addler, d c
Jacob Fink, d c
Jas Henderson, d c
A H Wenzle, d c
Michael Conrad, alien
Henry Haggerman, d c
Davik Paisely, o a
Wm J Montgomery, s d
John Reynolds d c
Geo W Leonard, d c
James Sutherland, d c
Levi Deroy, d c
Bartholomew Auth, d c
George Miller, alien
Christ Geisse, o a
Tim O'Leary, o a
Lawrence O'Connell, o a
Pat Russell, alien
John M'D Glenn, d c
Thos Pepperday, o a
Alex M Pollock, d c
Anthony Brun, o a
Saml Hesson, d c
Henry Haley, d c
Dennis M'Mullen, d c
Danl M'Mullen, d c
Jos Heastings, d c
Alex Potter, arsenal
Wm Murdock, alien

Wm P Richards, alien
David Steinheim, alien
Abram Lipner, d c
Lewis Aaron, alien
Daniel J Carroll, d c
Francis M'Laughlin, d c
Robt G Brinker p o clk
Thos M Coliff, o a
Wm Barry, o a
Jeremiah O'Brien, d c
John Kane, d c
Robert Munn, o a
Owen Owens, o a
Thomas Riley, alien
Michael Quinn, alien
Joseph Shoeb, d c
Robert Newell, alien
Edward Newell, alien
Michael Carroll, alien
James Tobin, d c
Michael Keefe, d c
Albert Jones, d c
Robeet Kirkpatrick, d c
Joseph Dougherty, d c
Michael Bagaley, alien
Michael Mead, d c
Patrick Guarin, d c
Augustus Kunz, alien
John Kroch, alien
Wm Newell, alien
Michael Keefe, d c
Jacob B Sigfried, d c
John L Pfeiffer, d c
Herman Schroeder, alien
Henry Schauderlein, alien
John D Thompson, d c
John Mullen, d c
Reuben Swain, o a
Dennis Sullivan, d c
Jeff Douglass, o a
B Rogers,   minister
Francis Edwards,   do
Andw M'Closkey,   do
Ianatus Trainor,   do
Philip Cassiday,   do
Anthony Gould,   do
Domenec Fleming,   do
John Fahey, alien
Wm Tully, alien
Michael Flannery, alien
Michael Melody, d c
Peter Fahey, alien
James Munson, alien
Patrick Price, alien
Isaac Pope, d c
M Ehrgott, d c
Thomas Donnelly, alien
Andrew Monahan, d c
John Sevelle, d c
Michael M'Graw, d c
Josep Linder, d c
Casper H Bruggeman, d c
Alex Morrison, d c
Francis Rooney, o a

Wm Matthews, alien
John Hannahan, alien
Bernard Rafferty, d c
Francis Gazzola, d c
Louis Cella, d c
Michael Cella, alien
Wm H Campbell, d c
Charles Nevue, d c
John Finnerty, o a
Patrick Shaughnossy, d c
John Robinson, d c
Thomas Kelly, d c
Philip Mertz, d c
Patrick Geoghegan, alien
Wm H Small, d c
Michael Coyle, d c
John J Gallagher, d c
Thos Pender, s d
Daniel Pender, eng'r
John B Eyth, d c
John Kenna, d c
Wm M'Bride, d c
John Finn, alien
Jas Dain, o a
Dennis Allen, d c
James Burns, d c
Wm Lindsey, o a
Matthew Bressner, d c
Thos Watt, n r
Robt M'Clelland, alien
Henry T Bowen, d c
Patrick Ward, alien
Jacob H Miller, d c
H Michels, mail carrier
Peter Madonnel, alien
Patrick M'Dermott, d c
Benj F Shueb, d c
Andrew Johnson, o a
Wm Ricketson, o a
A Frowenfeld, o a
Timothy Finin, d c
Gotleib Ludwig, d c
Math C Fullerton, d c
A C Ely, d c
John Mish, jr, d c
John Curran, d c
Wm A Halleck, d c
Joseph L Russell, o a
James Finch, d c
Daniel Fuller, d c
Jas S King, d c
Tim M'Carthy, o a
John M'Cann, o a
Timothy Sullivan, alien
John T Odam, o a
John Lowe, d c
Richard Sherridan, alien
Wm Bennett, d c
John Hart, alien
Chas W Lewis, s d
Thos Connor, o a
Alex Hunter, d c
Dennis Shannon, d c
Joseph D Herr, minister

Thomas B Hamilton, d c
Christian Kirchner, alien
Wm Kirchner, alien
S J Nolan, o a
A M'Cambridge, o a
Reinhart Ulrich, d c
John Hare, d c
Peter Schott, d c
Patrick Dunn, alien
Michl M'Laughlin, alien
Jos W Simonton, d c
Lawrence Ebbert, alien
Lewis Miller, o a
Daniel Donahue, d c
Julius Benstein, d c
Benj H Succop, o a
Fred Followay, alien
Myer Fink, d c
James Hague, alien
Adrian Siedle, alien

George Reineman, d c
Wm Stewart, d c
James Williams, d c
Jacob Klee, d c
Morris Flinn, d c
James Burke, alien
James O'Brian, d c
J G Seibenick, near sighted
Edwin Moreland, d c
Jas M'Closkey, o a
James Talbot, o a
John Douglas, minister
Wm Kroeger, alien
Peter Brady, s d
Patrick Dewyre, d c
Martin O'Connor, alien
Sampson Goldman, alien
Frederick Feldner, d c
Edward Devlin, d c
Charles J Wade, d c

John H Cassiday, o a
Thomas J Flood, deaf
Patrick Higgins, d c
Simon Johnston, d c
Joseph Seibert, d c
John Davis, alien
L Reineman, d c
James M'Kibben, d c
Henry Voskamp, d c
Wm M'Claren, o a
John R Voskamp, d c
James B Barr, d c
A H Thomas, minister
Jos Werckle, d c
Gotleib Ludwig, d c
John Curran, d c
Josesh Newell, d c
Casper Beman, d c
Joseph Shoeb, d c

FOURTH WARD.

Wm Drum, o a
John Martin, alien
John M'Kee, alien
Peter C Renier, d c
Dennis Martin, alien
Peter Nardie, alien
John Griffin, d c
W H Wortz, d c
Jos Frech, o a
Louis Pichard, d c
Thos Woods, d c
S Richards, d c
Max Hirsh, alien
John Fulton, d c
J Montgomery, d c
C Nordhein, alien
Jas M'Mahen, alien
A V Crouch, d c
W D Duffy, d c
David Agnew, d c
P M'Kenna, d c
D W Long, s d
James D Verner, d c
Michael Jones, o a
J S Gray, d c
L Gleisencamp, d c
Henry Happ, alien
Wm Colson, o a
Mark Hersh, alien
E S Warner, alien
Jas Laubie, d c
James Jones, d c
R Cunningham, d c
Matthew Smith, engineer
Thos Brown, d c

Chas Watt, o a
M Kern, alien
P H Stout, d c
D Fleming, o a
G W Treets, mail carrier
M Bentz, d c
Jos Lyons, alien
Wm Saddie, o a
J F Beckham, d c
James E Ross, d c
H R Long, d c
D Johnston, d c
R Cool, d c
Jake Walton, d c
Solomon Sbirey, d c
W N Chessman, o a
John Neeson, o a
W J Church, d c
Jas Parkinson, alien
H C T Lease, alien
H Bidwell, d c
A Frowenfeld, d c
W K M'Clintock, d c
L H Voight, d c
F E Chuffart, alien
Wm Sumner, d c
J Westbay, o a
John Duffy, o a
John Maffett, d c
M B Fetterman, d c
Jas Duffy, d c
Patrick Martin, alien
James Sweeny, alien
Morris M'Bride, d c
Pat Conoway, alien

Jas Dolan, o a
Jas Reed, alien
Pat Savage, d c
Thos Ryan, o a
H Oppenheimer, d c
E Lynch, o a
Wm Carson, d c
W Harman, d c
James Giniff, d c
Redmont G Ledlie, d c
John B Jones, d c
A T Schmidt, o a
L C Wilmarth, d c
G R Gardirce, d c
John Whalon, o a
Francis Whalon, alien
Isaac Abrams, d c
Julius Reisser, alien
Israel Rosenbloth, alien
Jacob Backrach, alien
Moses Oppenbeimer, alien
I Copelens, d c
Alex Walker, alien
James Gilnor, d c
C West, d c
M Hunnings, d c
Wm Roaney, d c
A O'Leary, d c
G F Shuchman, d c
James Clemens, alien
Mason Bavington, dis
G L B Fetterman, d c
Jason Noble, d c

FIFTH WARD.

Thomas Arnold, d c
James Alston, d c
Felix Ager, alien
Wm Adolph, en e
Alex Adams, o a
Barney Brean, d c
Joseph Brenstone, alien
Arthur Belk, alien
James Black, d c
Geo Brickner, o a
John Berger, d c
Peter Baker, dis
John Brown, dis
Geo Bader, d c
David Beck, d c
Richard Brengson, d c
Dorsey Bollow, eng
John Bruner, o a
James Bannon, d c
Nicholas Behr, d c
Janatius Balluf, alien
B B Bishop, d c
Jacob Brickner, alien
Alois Brickner, alien
James Bothwell, d c
Andy Boyd, d c
Thomas Brown, alien
George Bell, alien
John Bangart, d c
Thomas Boothe, d c
James Bennett, alien
E P Carr, d c
Henry Cleaver, d c
J O'Connor, o a
James Carr, d c
Robert Curry, d c
Thos Graham, alien
Henry Grine, d c
W G Griffith, alien
Wm Gallaher, d c
John Gelson, d c
Fred Heines, o a
John Henderson, o a
L Holtzman, d c
David Hays, alien
John Haffey, d c
J Helmproscht, minister
Geo Hemmer, d c
F H Hartman, en e
Julius Hoffman, alien
Jos Heckold, one leg off
Wm C Henney, eng
Peter Huelz, d c
Wm D Hamilton, d c
John Hodenfeitor, o a
David Hannah, en e
Peter A Heyer, d c
Anthony Huppy, o a
Timothy Haley, alien
Thos Hemlock, alien
John Jackson, d c

Clem Kesler, d c
James Kain, d c
Pat Kain, d c
Chas Kennedy, d c
W D Kearns, d c
Rudolph Kennich, alien
Chris Kountz, o a
G M Kaufman, alien
Wm Meik, alien
John Nelson, d c
Wm M Negley, en e
Wm Nelson, d c
Thos Newman, alien
David Nieman, alien
Henry Otte, d c
Pat O'Brien, alien
Wm O'Brien, alien
James Pillers, d c
Thos Parker, d c
Jos Putmeyer, d c
Thos D Patterson, d c
Barnard Poulich, alien
Wm Puter, d c
B Reahy, d c
Marker Rush, crippled
Jas Relley, arsenal
Fred Roxberry, alien
Henry Rule, d c
S B Reed, minister
W J Radcliff, d c
Peter Roth, d c
Thomas Stewart, alien
Robert Stevenson, alien
Wm Slack, alien
Isaac Sawyer, minister
Powell Schewl, alien
Geo Spear, d c
Geo Spratt, cripple
Adam Trap, d c
Felix C Negley, s d
Thomas Thompson, d c
Jos Thompson, d c
Edwd J Taylor, d c
Dan! Taylor, p o clerk
Bonaventure Zaringer, d c
M Glockner, alien
Wm Cook, alien, in the coun-
    try 18 years
Hiram Corant, d c
Danl Cornman, d c
James Carothers, o a
Saml Carothers, o a
Edwin Cohn, alien
August Clopfer, alien
F P Coffey, d c
James Colbert, d c
Arthur Carr, d c
M Connor, d c
James Creighton, d c
Michael Driscol, o a
Henry Dorncamp, alien

Richard Dean, o a
Louis Debitz, alien
Thomas Dain, o a
Henry Dunton, alien
Joseph Darrah, eng
Michael Dousley, alien
Franz Dorncamp, alien
John Dillon, o a
Sebastian Dorn, d c
Albert Evans, d c
Christ Evers, alien
Jacob Fogle, d c
Patrick Fitzpatrick, d c
R S Fergeson, eng
Lenhart Florich, alien
Peter Forsyth, d c
John Grein, alien
Jacob Godran, d c
Joseph Gress, alien
John Gemmer, d c
Wm Gray, eng
Henry Hunter, d c
Fred Kirsch, d c
Wm Kleinmons, d c
Abrah Katz, o a
John Kearns, d c
Wm Kirby, o a
David Kaye, o a
John Kamplouse, d c
Jackson Link, o a
Math Larimer, alien,
Jacob C Lang, d c
Adam Lauber, arsenal
Henry Leonard, alien
Joseph Lang, d c
Wm Leinlord, d c
J E Millenbraugh, alien
D F Malony, d c
Fred Miller, d c
Chas Meyers, d c
John Miller, d c
M'Connell Moore, en e
Arnold Miller, d c
Chris Menciner, d c
David Mitchell, d c
Wm Montooth, cripple
Thos Malony, d c
Wm Morgan, alien
Jacob Mixner, d c
Adam Milbert, d c
Mc McConnell, o a
Pat McCollough, d c
James McTighe, d c
Anthony McTighe, alien
Jas McKenna, d c
John Nihlstein, alien
Thos Ryree, d c
Jacob Rees, d c
David Richard, d c
Nic Snyder, d c
Joseph F Sower, alien

6   *List of Exempts.*

Anthony Springer, d c
Amond Shaffer, o a
Ebberhart Shibben, alien
Jacob Sower, alien
Robert Shuler, d c
Abraham Schlossberger, alien
Nic Seibert, d c
John Stroudenmeyer, d c
Sebastian Schultz, d c
John Supp, d c
John Sculley, alien

Isaac Snyder, eng
Richard Swaringen, o a
Saml Smith, crazy
Avin Schmidt, alien
Wm Stewart, d c
Peter Swan, alien
Joseph Schillinger, d c
David Thompson, d c
Jacob Utsler, o a
Martin Verzinger, dis
Thomas Wright, alien

J W Woodcock, arsenal
Jacob Weiget, minister
Thomas Whiteman, en e
Joachim Weisser, d c
John Wort, alien
Chas Wittinger, d c
Peter Winters, d c
Fred Wilharm, o a
Peter Wilson, alien
John Wood, alien
John Wiland, d c

SIXTH WARD.

William Hughes, alien
William White, dis
Robert Gibson, alien
James Casey, dec'd
Henry Till, dis
Hugh Rice, o a
Wm Walker, dec'd
Joseph Dougherty, dis
Anthony Heley, alien
Geo Bailey, arsenal
Oliver Brooks, dec'd
Danl Craig, alien
John H Johnston, dec'd
John Gittanan, d c
Thomas Edgar, alien
Nathaniel Nelson, d c
Michael Murphy, dis
Thos Hardy, alien
Alex M'Cracken, d c
Thomas Roberts, s d
John Wilson, d c
Wm Boland, d c
Saml Hobbs, d c
Wm M'Devitt, d c
Chas M'Devitt, d c
Wm Young, o a
Robt Flinn, o a
S H Stevenson, d c
Solomon Mumma, d c
Ernest Dietrich, d c
Jacob Deitrich, d c
Frederick Seigimer, d c
James Hopper, m d, alien
Westley Rutledge, d c
Saml Greer, o a
Robert M Carge, o a
Patrick Donahue, dis
John Wilson, d c
James Blackmore, d c
W F Murdock, o a
Abram Westervelt, d c
Chas Rossiter, d c
J Y M'Laughlin, o a
J R Niebaum, d c
Geo Berger, alien
Henry Backeldink, alien
D Z Brickell, s b captain
Chas B Mowry, eng
Joseph R Hughes, d c

Richard Jenkins, d c
John Rath, d c
Rush B Hawkins, d c
Adam Bell, alien
Thos Mulvehill, eng
John Bigly, eng
Jas M Vandegriff, c b clerk
Wm Myers, alien
Jas M'Cabe, d c
A Berkemeler, o a
Jesse Young, dis
Thos Miller, d c
T McGregor, mail carrier
G H Zackariah, o a
Fred Stetlander, d c
John Smith, d c
Saml A Hill, d c
Saml Ramsey, alien
David Edger, o a
Jas M'Kenney, d c
Valentine Sidney, d c
Wm Dodds, d c
A C McCallum, o a
Geo Wilson, o a
Steele Turbett, dis
Chas Neel, d c
Wm Shortel, d c
James M'Gregor, d c
Wm Rossiter, d c
S L Burnap, d c
W Collingwood, o a
Edmund Grier, o a
W C Stewart, d c
H H Truby, d c
Wm Guimme, alien
John Cook, d c
Anderson Hagan, o a
John Phillips, s d
John Scott, o a
F Sullivan, o a
Thos Rafferty, alien
Wm Smith, d c
Thos Kelly, o a
Patrick O'Hara, o a
Reuben King, d c
F J Ribbeck, alien
Jas Bowden, d c
Geo Arnold, o a
Alex Shank, d c

John Sherman, d c
F Thompson, dis
Fred Suck, d c
Robert Coyle, d c
J P Smith, eng
H Lambert, o a
James Sahl, d c
Geo W Verner, dis
F H Bushman, d c
Wm Cluley, d c
J M Burns, o a
H K Colton, d c
H H Niebaum, d c
N Swartzelder, o a
Edward Duncan, alien
Michael Shannon, arsenal
H R Geilfuss, d c
John H Succup, d c
Alfred Wright, d c
Patrick Murphy, d c
Joseph Writer, d c
Anthony Fretig, o a
Francis Buskuff, d c
Barney Sander, d c
E Buhtold, d c
Chas Martin, o a
Patrick Burke, o a
Henry Millen, o a
Alex Seaner, d c
John Row, d c
John Kirkpatrick, dis
George Culp, o a
John Keife, o a
Wm M'Gill, d c
James Graham, o a
Archibald Wallace, d c
Levi Dillow, d c
Ebenezer M'Knight, d c
James Murray, o a
Benj M'Guire, o a
Frank Conley, d c
Burwell Hunnicut, d c
Wm M'Adams, dis
James M'Closkey, eng
Robert Fleming, alien
Stephen Keef, d c
Henry Cluley, d c
Wm Backindick, alien
Christian Kruse, d c

John Rebman, d c
William H Whitney, d c
Robt Moffit, sr, o a
James Stewart, alien
R Seidle, d c
C A Ammon, d c
George Armor, dis
Graham Scott. s d
Wm Wilson, d c
J H Niebaum, d c
Wm Gleen, d c
Hugh Campbell, d c
Patk O'Leary, o a
Wm H Ebbert, d c
Geo Henly, alien
E C Smigt, d c
Francis M'Graw, d c
Francis W Cluley, d c
Henry Gaw, alien
Jas Lindsey, o a
Theo Woods, d c
Wash Gallagher, dis
James C Elliot, eng
A Hosman, o a

Wm Vietmer, d c
John Walters, alien
S W Owens, d c
George H Thurston, d c
Joseph Shaepaner, d c
John Hamon, o a
Conrad Shipp, dis
F D Giest, d c
H Gordon, dis
Wm Martin, o a
Theo Snyder, alien
Joseph Hardy. d c
R R Garrison, dis
Alex M'Ilwain, d c
John Miller, o a
A J Foster, o a
James Kelly, o a
James Harding, d c
J A Cochran, d c
J Althouse, o a
John Kern, d c
Steven McIlwaine, d c
Wm Farley, dis
Matthew Carrell, d c

Matthew Carrell, jr, dis
Edward Nugent, alien
Wm Hays, d c
James Kennedy, d c
Richard Keefe, o a
Francis Goodwin, d c
Richard Hinds, o a
Morris Marra, alien
Brant Shannon, dis
Frank Brady, d c
Lewis Allen, d c
Samuel Logan, dis
Joseph Patterson, alien
James Kinlon, o a
James Gilmore, eng
L Patterson, eng
John Park, o a
Michael Grant, alien
Wm J Wilson, d c
Henry Herd, d c
John Eness, d c
Geo Tanner, dis
Geo B M'Kee, o a
R M'Adams, o a

SEVENTH WARD.

Francis Allen, o a
Wm Edmonds, alien
Henry Boden, d c
Ed Bryce, d c
Danl Coleman, alien
Jas Cattemole, o a
Matthew Crawford, alien
Ed W Doty, s d
James Kastley, d c
Henry Eairing, d c
Jas B Fleming, d c
Thos Gibson, o a
John Groatzinger,
Chris Harlow, alien
Geo Hubely, o a
Wm Hannon, d c

Wm Jackson, d c
Patrick Kerr, d c
Fred Kraff. d c
Thos Kraff, o a
Henry Lingerfelter, d c
James L Walles, alien
John Lippincott, d c
Stewart M'Kee, o a
Patrick M'Stein, o a
George M'Clowry, d c
Joseph Myers, d c
Chas Meyran, d c
Edward M'Govern, d c
Geo B Miller, o a
Andrew Nesbit, arsenal
Noah Potts, eng

James Pownell, arsenal
Theo Patterson, pilot
John Puricher, o a
Conrad Robb, d c
Chas A Shafer, d c
Henry Snively, s d
John P Shall. d c
Augustus Siefert, pilot
James Sewall, alien
John Sweeny, o a
Ben Turner, d c
Job Whitell, d c
David Wesler, d c
John Coyne, d c
Thos Keef, o a

EIGHTH WARD.

James Corbett, d c
Crawford Armstrong, d c
J Devine, d c
J Carey, alien
R Jones, d c
Pat May, o a
James Watson, d c
Edward Hutchison, d c
D Quinlin, d c
A Byrne, alien
John Mullin, d c
James Rodgers, d c
J M'Guire, alien
James Brown, alien
John Quigley, alien
Thomas Connor, alien

Evan Evans, alien
Anthony Farrell, alien
James M'Garvy, d c
Thos Snowden, eng
J P Estep, d c
Albert Windburst, d c
J D Fackiner, alien
Patrick Byrne, o a
W H Devore, d c
P Duffy, alien
Wm Burns, d c
P Coyne, d c
L Sweeny, alien
T Johnson, eng
Squire Cook, d c
Wm Zimgan, d c

Robert Weinder, d c
J Kerr, d c
J Hannen, d c
Pat Hannen, d c
Barny Kane, d c
J M'Avoy, alien
W Reamen, d c
T Neely, s d
J A Kaercher, d c
J L Hamilton, s d
Fred Shroeder, d c
Chris W Smith, d c
D Day, o a
Pat Harper, d c
Joseph Adams, d c
Chris Shultz, d c

Stephen Dobbins, d c
Manus M'Fadelin, alien
T O'Hara, alien
F Whiting, d c
J M'Quilin, alien
M Farrell, alien
Peter M'Quillin, d c
J Kitz, d c
J Daugherty, d c
G Rache, d c
J Adams, d c
H B Beazele, eng
Chris Christy, d c
Mich Sullivan, alien
James White, d c
Henry Rebel, alien
J H Stevenson, d c

P Killillay, alien
B Haley, alien
Wm M'Garvey, d c
John Hook, d c
Fred Bowman, d c
Louis Berkowitz, d c
Aug Reossler, d c
Jacob Cashbaun, d c
Geo Younger, d c
Henry Walker, alien
Hugh M'Master, d c
Wm Anderson, d c
Jas S Black, dis
Jas S Wright, dis
Fred Doerr, dis
John Hugo, d c
R Keef, o a

John Kerr, o a
J Ammon, d c
Peter Kaltenfern, dis
Jacob Rosenwig, o a
Ernest Sagaman, d c
Thos Conlon, d c
John M Killen, d c
H H D Armon, d c
H B Brocket, d c
Peter Weldon, d c
Fred Weigandt, d c
Edw Rutledge, d c
Wm Coleman, d c
T Buetyon, teacher
Anthony Byrne, eng

NINTH WARD.

Stephen Baker, alien
Edward Barber, alien
Francis Newmont, eng
Martin Campbell, d c
Jacob Leise, d c
Jacob Bartlett, o a
Arch Gilmore, eng
Joseph Pressell, d c
James M'Caffrey, d c
Robt Hughes, d c
Jos Bollman, arsenal
Jno T Bear, d c
Wm Ott, eng
Jas Wright, o a
Michael Zeek, d c
Danl Dick, eng
Chas Parkin, alien
Jos B Cherry, d c
Edwd J Hughes, d c
Louis Walter, arsenal
Thos M'Connell, alien
Danl Colbert, d c
Wm Cain, d c
Jacob F Geist, alien
John Lutz, dis
John Ridley, eng
Louis Walthour, eng
Augustus Wentz, d c
James Smith, eng
Wm Kerr, d c
Hiram Engler, en e
David Kerr, eng
Henry Hudson, eng
Jacob Frankhouser, eng
Phillip Klingermau, eng
Watson Campbell, eng
Joseph Hood, en e
John Widinthal, d c
Richard Allen, eng
Wm C Johns, d c
William Evans, alien
Edward Kenna, o a
James O'Rourke, eng

Wm Jones, eng
Joseph L Roberts, d c
James Lees, alien
Wm Kenworthy, alien
John Brown, d c
Joseph H Nobbs, s d
Wm Holroyd, d c
Danl Colclasser, en e
Thos Shriver, d c
John Welsh, s d
James Horacks, d c
Fred Fleck, eng
Harry Elliot, dis
Wm Wills, eng
George F Irwin, eng
F M De Armitt, dis
Jacob Angus, eng
William A Pitzer, en e
Alexander Boyce, dc
William Dixon, alien
John Carson, alien
Edward Stewart, d c
J Klingensmith, engineer
C B Holmer, d c
James Neeson, d c
Robert Bond, d c
William Lingell, d c
Shultz Spellman, engineer
Frederick Dobbenmyer, d c
Samuel Robinson, d c
Andrew Dobbenmyer, d c
Frederick Rommell, d c
Alexander Hannah, d c
Nicholas Stipple, d c
Patrick Cook, alien
Martin Nichol, alien
L Falkenhagen, d c
Joseph Bergoon, d c
John Major, engineer
M Sweeny, engineer
William Williams, engineer
Rich'd O' Connor over age
David Connell, alien

Wm Sontag, d c
Henry Yerkins, d c
David Dillon, alien
Peter Costello, eng'r
Thos Hinds, d c
Elias Peak, d c
John Murray, d c
John Drummond, d c
Thos Ball, alien
Phillid Dahlen, d c
George Mullen, d c
Jas F Martin, d c
Robert Sproul, d c
Joseph Fehrer, d c
James Bourke, alien
Jocob Staub, d c
Thos Grogan, over age
Vincent M' Gadden, d c
Louis Berger, alien
Tomes Littell, s d
Joseph Irwin, d c
John Tibby, 31 years in country, alien
Jacob Alters, d c
John Lowe, alien
Henry Kouverman, d c
Henry Rurga, over age
Frederick Dietman, d c
Richard Birkeybile, d c
John M'Intyre, d c
Robert Algeo, d c
David Wallaker, d c
Augustus Wolf, eng
John Harrison, s b
Abraham Campbell, d c
R P Hare, en e
Wm Hudson, en e
Saml B M' Keugh, eng
Edward Barten, d c
Wm Gebbart, d c
Isaac Walters, dis
Jacob Wingard, d c
John S Miller, s d

Michael Bright, d c
Hugh Diamond, d c
Henry Allen, alien
John White, alien
Reub Massailon, over age
C Simmerman, alien
Edward Landy, dis
Edward Layton, eng
John Albneght, d c
Joseph L Havins, d c
James Carroll, over age
Thomas M' Donald, d c

Samual Dougerty, dis
William Burns, alien
Samuel Geer, d c
E Derar, eng
Thos Wilson, eng
Luman Rogers, d c
Jas Robinson, d c
Jos Paterson, over age
Mathew Connell, d c
Chas Rethmiller, d c
Wesley Greir, d c
Jas Potts, over age

G Leguillen, d c
Benj Naylor, alien
Wm Johnston, d c
E Grifflth, over oge
Theo Powers, m c
Henry Cassidy, eng
Davis Minster, eng
Sam Dougerty, dis
David Campbell
Jaseph Cullen, d c
John Stormer, d c
Martin Bracken, en e

ALLEGHENY.

FIRST WARD.

Henderson Wiley, eng
Wm A Charlton, dis
James Bell, eng
John Agy, eng
John Ragen, pilot
Wm Campbell, dis
Pat L Ward, d c
C J F Buckley, alien
John Walsh, d c
Sam Riddle, postmaster
Geo N Miller, eng
Sam R Davis, d c
Wm Fish, pilot
George W Moore, eng
T Costamagna, pensn'r

John Shearer, d c
Sol Joseph, alien
John Kitchen, over age
Ed Butten, over age
George Alexander, d c
Sam Peacock, alien
Stephen Kindle, alien
Jesse Robinson, tel operator
William E Cowell, do
William Lloyd, alien
James Patten, alien
Henry Lank, d c
Charles Tuttle, dis
David Acor, d c
Wm McCune, alien

James McCune, alien
James F Reno, d c
Henry Naughton, alien
Lewis Reno, pilot
Robt M Boles, pilot
Thomas Sanders, d c
Wm P Bardell, d c
George W Lyon, d c
Thos H Bew, alien
Charles A Hodgkiss, d c
Leonard McCandless, tel op
Edward Barr, d c
James Oldden, dis

SECOND WARD.

And M Matthews, d c
Walter Thompson, alien
Sam Brown, alien
John Philron, d c
H D Reymer, d c
John Magoffin, d c
Alexander Taylor, d c
Wm W Martin, over age
John Hazlett, pilot
Wm H Smith, d c
John Sullivan, d c
George W Reed, over age
George Gipner, d c
Wm A Lee, over age
Henry Dalmyer, d c

John Husler, eng
Wm Mahoon, d c
S D King, eng
Charles Dallmeyer, d c
Thomas Pratt, d c
Josiah Lowe, alien
Harris Babcock, d c
Samuel Parker, alien
John Grant, d c
Patrick Campbell, alien
James Powell, d c
David Ross, engineer
Wm Sprague, engineer
James Simpson, d c
Joseph Ross, engineer

Benj J Haddington, d c
James Hamilton, pilot
David Hunter, d c
Wm Park, d c
Samuel Crow, d c
Archibald Richey, eng'r
Benj Hawk, d c
Levi Clouser, d c
Charles Rice, d c
Ebenezer Searle, d c
Henry Ackley, d c
J O S Golden, d c
James Orr, d c
John R Garrett, eng'r
J W Roberts, d c

Wm Cooven, engineer
Wm Bergoyne, d c
John Wilson, alien
Erastus Gray, eng
II C Richmond, eng
P G Ellings, d c
T F Grubbs, d c
Chas H Cutler, d c
John Lane, d c
Geo McKnight, alien
Henry Corman, d c
Jesse K Scott, d c
J L Smith, p o clerk
C R Church, eng
John L Crawford, d c
Richard Pegg, alien
Alexander Leech, over age
William Gee, over age

Henry Wymend, d c
Hugh Johnston, eng
Henry Israel, eng
Oliver Feecher, over age
John Whitehead, alien
David Dorman, eng
Michael Murphy, alien
John Martin, alien
Michael A Barnes, d c
Edward Upstill, d c
F M Cooley, engineer
Emanuel Greenwalt, alien
Joseph Allender, d c
Francis Murray, engineer
John C Anderson, d c
Owen Gogens, alien
Thomas Lucy, d c
Daniel Lucy, alien

David Dennison, d c
Samuel Wheeler, d c
James J Scott, engineer
John Hunter, alien
Wm West, alien
John Campbell, d c
John Turmile, alien
James C Brown, d c
George Kimberlin, alien
John Arbuckle, engineer
Charles Huzzard, engineer
P Reymer, d c
Jeremiah Galerest, d c
Richard Higgen, d c
Thomas Brady, alien
Henry Merrick, d c
C W Ramsey, engineer

THIRD WARD.

Thomas Miller, d c
John Peters, d c
H Hockstein, d c
Fred Zetum, d c
Anthony Longbitz, alien
Fred Keizler, d c
Thos J Blake, dis
Constant Fry, d c
John J Hackstine, d c
John Steirbalm, d c
Herman Beck d c
Fred Bluckbaum, d c
Baltzer Stephen, over age
Charles Fisher, alien
Noah Myers, d c
Fred Ibendahl, over age
Augustus Walter, d c
Charles Frick, dis
Lewis Shaffer, alien
John P Wacker, d c
Isaac Rhode, d c
John Hartman, d c
Joseph Smith, d c
Peter Shatz, d c
Martin Schafer, d c
Joseph Salim, d c
Jos Hookensteine, alien
Arthur M'Ginn, d c
Fred Schwartz, d c
Christian Kilf, d c
Francis Ratzell, d c
John W Duvall, eng
William Morrison, d c
John C Morrison, d c

Dennis M'Eleer, d c
George Sims, over age
William Gilland, d c
Wm J Ford, engineer
Benj Ford, engineer
Simon Kaufman, d c
Jas Middleburg, d c
Lewis Kall, d c
Francis Spect, d c
Samuel Dicker, d c
John Carson, alien
Robt H White, teacher
David Moon, d c
Serren Yenson, alien
Henry Walter, alien
Matthew Kimm, d c
William Conkle, d c
John Wolf, d c
Chas Geltman, d c
Thomas York, d c
Chas Hawthorne, engineer
Samuel McKibben, alien
Peter Smith, d c
John Van Horn, d c
Wm Fairley, alien
Fred King, alien
Samuel Linham, alien
Robert Elton, d c
Wm Fanghender, engineer
Andrew J Gordon, d c
Benj F Woodburn, min
Alexander McIntosh, alien
Wm H Edie, d c
Wm K Gray, d c

James B Edie, over age
Edward Price, non res
John Caldwell, engineer
James H Sewell, over age
Carney McCartney, alien
Joseph McNaugber, d c
Gerhard E Moran, d c
John Dalzell, alien
Ludwig Schuler, d c
Henry Stebbing, d c
John Farrell, d e
John White, d c
Thomas York, d c
David W Morris, d c
Jacob Sturkle, d c
Wm J Herron, over age
Hugh Knox, alien
William P Torrence, d c
V B McGahen, over age
Louis Kall, d c
George Stoolfire, d c
Harmon Harsh, alien
Moses Arnold, alien
William Richey, alien
Philotus Dean, minister
John Fitzsimmons, d c
Leonard K Knapp, d c
John Williamson, d c
John L Kerr, pilot
A Gugenheimer, d c
Jas P Fleming, p d
Eli Meanor, d c

FOURTH WARD.

Charles Green, alien
John Kennedy, alien
John Graham, not a citizen
Robert Johnston, alien

Quinton Casselbery, tel o
Robert Knox, alien
Charles Frinklebosh, d c
John Walkinshaw, alien

John Hawthorn, alien
Wm Hawthorn, alien
Robt Hawthorn, alien
Philip Hoffman, d c

Jacob Meyer, d c
John Elliott, alien
Patrick Cunningham, d c
Francis Huggins, d c
Jno Hoffman, blind, right eye
George Urban, d c
Robert Maxwell, d c
Wm Boley, en e
Henry Redman, d c
Casper Weyman, d c
George Wirt, d c
John Bleakley, dis
J J McDermott, en e
B F Adams, d c
Robt Armstrong, n r—paroled by rebels
Francis Thompson, d c
Anthony Enning, d c
J N Ziegler, dis
J P Johnston, d c
J S Willock, d c
James Bradley, alien
Wm Olney, over age
A Levi, alien
John Woolen, dis
John Thompson, dis
S B Robinson, d c
R C Stevenson, d c
W L Harper, d c
Samuel McCowan, d c
Charles F Tutter, d c
William Cox, d c
Richard Johnston, alien
J S Orton, dis
James Felter, dis
James Pauline, dis
John Bodarmy, dis
Wm Bearhorst, dis
Michael Sour, d c
J F Rabe, d c
Joseph Champion, d c
James F Tompkins, dis
Conrad Ahliere, alien
John Thoma, alien
Joseph Thoma, alien
William Merriman, d c

James Sterling, d c
William Bender, d c
Patrick O'Hanlon, alien, 14 years in the country
James Hulliehin, d c
Robert Matthias, d c
William Varnum, d c
Christian Wolf, alien
John Mitsch, d c
George Juengert, d c
J. Baldinger, d c
Henry Schulz, d c
W E Kahler, minister
George Nixon, d c
J S Pierson, d c
Augustus Ferst, alien
C R Carlyle, d c
James Colley, alien
James McElroy, d c
Alexander McElroy, d c
James Coil, alien
Samuel Palmer, d c
John N Glogger, alien
John Gum, d c
T J Munden, d c
John Maclain, jr., d c.
Abraham Faust, over age
Samuel Lambert, dis
Herman Handel, d c
Jas A Thompson, alien
E F Boyd, d c
J J East, d c
Thomas Rhodes, dis
C McIntyre, alien
W N Howard, d c
Robert Hadfield, alien
William Gullyes, alien
Robert Walters, dis
W H Robinson, d c
James Robinson, d c
R B Sterling, d c
James Gault, d c
Thos C Wilson, engineer
Wm McFadden, alien
James Clark, alien
J H Tompkins, dis

John Hazlett, jr., d c
John Titzell, d c
Louis Glaser, d c
George Myers, d c
G H Bollman, alien
Louis Richards, alien
Isaac Collins, d c
J V Link, alien
John Metzenbaker, d c
Benj A Robinson, dis
Valentine Christman, d c
E C Rotzsell, d c
Frank Pilgrim, d c
James Milligan, d c
Amos Suthen, dis
John Beck, dis
Samuel Haney, dis
Allen Faust, deaf
Herman Miller, d c
John Kahner, d c
James Haneyman, alien
Francis Mackle, d c
Rinehart Buck, alien
George Miller, d c
John Boles, d c
Geo Kleggenhoffer, d c
Andrew Klinance, d c
Joseph Wolfe, d c
George Repuch, d c
Thomas Cutter, d c
Peter Bradle, d c
Louis Beckholt, alien
Samuel Hadfield, over age
William Curry, d c
John McCune, alien
Hurcules McCord, d c
J G M'Connell, d c
George Holdship, d c
P G Weichert, d c
James Hill, d c
George Killen, alien
J C Stephenson, d c
H A Coffin, d c
William Irwin, alien.

BOROUGHS.

EAST BIRMINGHAM.

John Ralzer, d c
Frank Raumgardon, d c
H Vor der Bruecke, d c
Goerge Porester, d c
John Wintergill, d c
J N Laborser, d c
Gregor Fox, d c
J Q A Barnes, d c
Amsly Smith, d c
John Hughes, s d
Joseph J Ulam, d c
John Snyder, d c
David Challinor, d c
Frank Plunkett, d c
John Herron, lost an arm at Drainesville,
John Osingar, been in U. S. since 1846 and says he is not a citizen
N Keller. d c
Thomas Wallace, d c
Chas W Hamilton, d c
John A Wenzel, d c
Francis Blood, over age
Wm Smith, engineer
John U Miller, alien
Edward Anthony, alien
Peter Bloobinger, dis
C J Schullz, d c
Andrew Nann, d c
Jacob Schook, engineer

N H Plummer, s d
Wm Lips, d c
George Link, dis
C A Church, engineer
Adam Weyman, d c
George Geyer, d c
M Kappler, dis
Jacob Krumm, d c
J A H Carson, d c
Patrick Keating, alien
George W Jones, p m
Lewis Schaler, p o clerk
Henry Buddy, d c
Patrick Pierce, d c
Wallace Gardner, d c
John Whinton, d c
Gustave Espy, lame leg
Aug Ammond mail car
Michael Keck, dis
T Carnahan, bad eyes
William Harris, d c
Wm Blackson, d c
Alex Dowden, d c
S Vanderan, lost a hand
John Schuman, dis
John N Forger, d c
Frank Stewart, d c
B Rust, d c
William Rosser, d c
Jones Jones, d c
Alexander Mowry, d c

John Lebner, dis
H Hebrauk, d c
Wm Mittenzwei, s d
R D Brice, d c
Dennis Riley, d c
Joseph Gettler, alien
Levi Schook, engineer
Wm Evans, d c
A Dougherty, dis
James Gibson, alien
Wm Scott, alien
Alex Patton, dis
John Beer, d c
Chas Stolzenbach, d c
Dominic Ihmsen, d c
Robert Taw, d c
M Church, d c
John Fink, d c
Henry Sounenschem, d c
P Euler, d c
John Giser, dis
Fred Shuttle, d c
Phillip Zell, d c
Dennis M'Carthy, alien
P Helmlinger, alien
John Phillips, d c
T O Hughard, d c
John Lauth, d c
Joseph Walton, s d

LAWRENCEVILLE.

Henry Ahlburn, s d
Wm H Andrews, min
Geo W Barr, d c
John Bair l, d c
Fred Blackhouse arsenal
Henry Becker, arsenal
M Blankinpeler, alien
Kearnes Bracken, d c
Alex C Bell, d c
Wm Brown, arsenal
Under Cooper, alien
Samuel Colvin, d c
James Cinnamon, d c
Charles De Knight, s d
John Daniels, d c
Wm Deume, alien
John Dunn, d c
John B Earl, d c
Adam Esler, engineer

Wm B Edwards, arsenal
T J Ellwood, arsenal
Robert Esler, arscual
Wm Foster, alien
Agustus Hoyer, d c
Thos J Hunter, over age
Boniface Hess, arsenal
Edw Horting, arsenal
William Hall, arsenal
Lewis Holland, arsenal
Wm H Huber, arsenal
John Herman, alien
Henry Haer, arsenal
Wm J Hastings, dis
Jackson Hull, d c
Chas F Hughes, m c
George Hall, arsenal
Wm H Hull, arsenal
Wm Hoffstadt, arsenal

Christ Irwin, arsenal
James Johnston, arsenal
Mathew Jordan, d c
Francis Jeffrey, arsenal
John Jackson, arsenal
Wm Kenworthy, d c
Wm M'Conehue, arsenal
John M'Kee, alien
C C Middlebaugh, arsenal
Jno R M'Laughlin arsenal
Jos Matthews, arsenal
John Mullen, arsenal
Robert Martin, arsenal
John M'Dormott, d c
H W Myers, d c
Johr. M' Conagby, arsenal
Jas R Murphy, d c
Michael Mackey, arsenal
Wm Montooth, arsenal

Thos Mulvany, arsenal
Dennis Malony, arsenal
R L Miller, minister
George M'Neely, arsenal
Alex Moriety, d c
John T Means, d c
Conrad Malcus, alien
Michael J M' Cann, d c
John Mitchell, d c
Pat Melville, arsenal
Jas E M'Clure, arsenal
Patrick M'Graw over age
Hugh Mackey, d c
Patrick M' Quillen, alien
Mathew Riccards, alien
Wm Ryan, arsenal
Edwin Ruddenbaugh, arsenal
Wm Stuchfield, m c
Wm Smulstack, arsenal
Aug. Smith, arsenal
Wm Sword, arsenal
John Schofield, arsenal
John Scott, alien
Jas M Snowden, en e
Robt A Scott, dis
John Stewart, alien
David Stofiel, d c
Edwin Sherrett, d c
John Snaffer, d c
Henry Stimel, arsenal
Geo Schluderberg, arsenal
W M Wilson, arsenal
John V Wharton, arsenal
Reuben Williamson, alien
Moiety Fredericks, alien
John B Flender, arsenal
T Fay, alien
James Fenton, arsenal
John Featherline, alien
Jas Fondersmith, arsenel
Martin V B Fowler, arsenal
Anthony Fisher, arsenal

Geo Fox, arsenal
David Freeman, dis
Daniel Farrel, arsenal
Henry Frank, arsenal
John Foight, arsenal
Daniel French, arsenal
Joseph Grim, arsenal
Joseph Grier, arsenal
A A Gilbert, arsenal
Hugh Grunt, arsenal
David Goff, arsenal
F Ferdinand, d c
Casper Gilbert, arsenal
Adam Hoffman, arsenal
Peter Hoarr, arsenal
Charles Haid arsenal
Charles King, arsenal
Peter Kirk, arsenal
Samuel King, arsenal
William Keenan, dis
Christ Knauer, arsenal
George Krause, d c
Charles Kline, arsenal
Herman Keller, arsenal
John Kerny, alien
Thos Kennedy, arsenel
John P Knaur, arsenal
Wm Kroning, arsenal
John Keplinger, arsenal
Arthur Kelloway, arsenal
Thomas Laly, arsenal
Uriah Laughlin, arsenal
Michl Lovegate, arsenal
Joseph Lemon, arsenal
Fredk Letzkus, arsenal
James Lyons, arsenel
John F Leipfarth, arsenal
Chris Lenkhardt, arsenal
John Longstaff, arsenal
J W Lewkins, arsenal
Francis M' Gowder, arsenal
Wm M' Cutcheon, arsenal

Saml M' Mahan, s d
Patrick Martin, d c
Patrick M' Quillen, d c
Jacob Metz, arsenal
John M' Whinney, arsenal
Jos Montgomery, arsenal
Wm Mitchell arsenal,
O S Middlekauff, arsenal
Michl Neckerman, arsenal
Melchl'ck Nailer, alien
Henry Nailor, alien
Henry Nasser, d c
N H Norfolk, arsenal
John Orth, arsenal
Wm Obie, m c
Augustus Pferdort, d c
Jno E Patton, arsenal
Theo Powers, en e
Wm Phillips, arsenal
John Rodolph, d c
Thos Ross, arsenal
Samual W Reynolds, d c
Levi Remree, arsenal
Geo S Richmond, arsenal
Oliver P Woods, arsenal
Robt C Woods, arsenal
John Wells, arsenal
John Wolf, arsenal
John Leese, arsenal
Jos B Thomas, arsenal
Thos Hopkins, alien
C R Thomas arsenal
Lewis Unverzaght, d c
W H Williams, d c
And. West, arsenal
E W Wright, arsenal
Wm Vernon, arsenal
Robt Young, arsenal
Jacob Young, arsenal
Nich Yerger, arsenal
Zach Zacharias, alien
Joseph Zuck, m c

BIRMINGHAM.

Oliver M'Shane, d c
Job Winfield, alien
David Deaker, d c
David Slack, alien
Isaac Williams, alien
John Bottles, d c
Wm Wilson, d c
August Rose, d c
Oswald Keller, d c
Isaac Hixenbaugh, d c
John F Reed, o a
John J Greot, en e
John Sbomaker, d c
Evan Finch, d c
Thos Bevington, d c
Dominick Cunningham, d c
Herman Long, d c
Wm Barr, engineer

Nick Kountzler, d c
Jno G Herbel, d c
Louis Weber, d c
Chas Ohliger, o a
Evan J Davis, alien
Emanl Schell, o a
Jno Carrick, d c
Jno Stewart, alien
Thos Ward, d c
Jno Zweldinger, d c
Daniel Wenke, p m
Henry Hermire, alien
Stephen Struntz, d c
Jacob J Vandergrift, d c
John Wilson, alien
Jas Shepherd, alien
Matthew Berry, d c
Wash M'Kee, d c

Cornelius Hays, alien
Geo Duncan, d c
Wm Vogen, en e
A C Donalson, en e
Edward Moya, d c
Patrick Coyle, en e
Edward Cooper, d c
Daniel Gross, d c
Henry Bearman, d c
Leopold Och, d c
Fred Deither, minister
Charles Edwards, alien
Anth Sneizbour, alien
Anthony Urbans, d c
Jas B Evans, d c
John M'Allister, alien
Joseph Pleger, d c
Timothy Heft, d c

Philip Osprion, d c
Christian Brill, d c
Sebastian Pope, alien
Chas Miller, d c
Dan Stewart, alien

Pius Souder, deaf
Jno P Beech, asst p o
P D Liscomb, o a
Henry Fern, alien
Geo Vaux, engineer

Isaac B Jacobs, d c
David Evans, alien
David Brenniman, pilot
Jno Brecht, d c

MANCHESTER.

B A Samson, s d
Alex M'Kee, d c
Thos Duffy, eng'r
Andrew Mulides, o a
John T Wright, eng'r
John W Gardiner, eng'r
Chas F Irvin, d c
Wm S Graham, eng'r
James Atkinson, eng'r
Joseph Goodwin, d c
Thos Miller, eng'r
James M Cornwell, s d
Joseph Hall, d c

Milton Woods, eng'r
Edward M'Chamber, eng'r
Henry Faulkner, s d
Amos Bryan, dis
Wm Johnston, d c
Wm Howard, alien
Byron L Beden, eng'r
Thomas Everson, d c
R Fearbley, eng'r
Thomas Johnston, alien
Edmond Hays, alien
James Rodgers, d c
Peter Householder, eng'r

James H Logan, eng'r
Jeremiah Mosher, m c
Joseph Cadwick, s d
Morris V Miller, eng'r
Cornelius Murdock, d c
Benj Fowler, d c
Samuel M'Cune, s d
John T Reno, pilot
Joseph Harper, dis
Caleb Parr, d c
George Peyton, eng'r
Wm A Porter, eng'r
Wm Carmichael, alien

SOUTH PITTSBURG.

Thos Blackmore, dis
Michael Brecht, dis
Chas Bausman, dis
Sidney J Brauff, dis
Jos Betsler, d c
Jacob Blatch, dis
Hugh Chambers, d c
Robt Creighton, d c
James Cready, s d
James Deithoon, d c
Timothy Doyle, alien
Hiram Daily, dis
Wm Edwards, d c
John Forsyth, dis
Henry Fork, d c

John Hollenback, d c
D R Jones, alien
David C Kerr, pilot
Geo Konn, d c
Wm Lenz, d c
David Lloyd, o a
Jacob Murphy, dis
Bernard Marl, d c
James M'Keever, alien
Thos M'Keever, alien
Jas M'Clelland, dis
Nelson J M'Kinney, d c
Wm M'Dowell, alien
Robt Neely, jr, dis
Andrew Oyer, d c
A O'Donnell, eng'r

Isaac Phillips, o a
Jos Richards, d c
Geo D Sharp, s d
Wash Stanley, dis
Jacob Smith, d c
Frank Sprew, d c
Peter Slicker. d c
David Scott, alien
Philip Snewer, d c
Jacob Fracts, d c
Jones Unks, dis
August Vietmier, d c
Nich Wieland, d c
M Winterbalter, d e
Geo Yeager, d c

TEMPERANCEVILLE.

John Antwerpan, d c
Asoph Broad, dis
Geo R Cochran, d c
Maloky Connelly, alien
Jas Carroll, n r
Henry Esplen, s d
Thos Ferguson, d c

Geo K Gamble, s d
David Henderson, d c
Even Jones, dis
James D Koons, d c
John Murray, d c
M M'Grannier. dis
Wm Nesbitt, arm off
Leander Robinson, dep Reg'r

W J Richardson, Register of
　Allegheny Co
David Sobinson, s d
Wm M Simcox, s d
James Wallace, cripple
Wm Wirts, d postmaster
Wm Chew, cripple

TARENTUM.

P G Bell, minister
Saml Ramsey minister
J H Yemmonds, minister
Joseph Horne, minister
Danl Roush, demented
Saml Bagaley, dis

Alex Hazlett, blind of one eye
Robert Miller, s d
E M M'Call, d c
Chris Mauxhunur, alien
J M Porter, s d
L M Stephens, s d

John Snyder, alien
Hezekiah Vantine, alien
Danl Yancy, alien
Henry Seelhorst, alien
G W Hazlett, dis

DUQUESNE.

Conrad Bricknor, alien
George Ball, alien
John Ball, alien
Wm T Barkley, dis
Ph'lip Babbinger, alien
John C Ehrner, d c
Ernest Egners, jr, d c
Wm Finley, alien
Hugh Garrigan, alien, 10 years in the country

Gottfried Fischer, dis
Christopher Grutz, d c
Budd Gaskill, d c
Andrew Hepp, alien
Andrew Hare, s d
John Johnston, dis
Summerville Keep, dis
Henry B Lyon, d c
Edward Miller, d c
James Murphy, d c

Robert M'Connell, d c
Wm Oakley, s d
Wayne Ramsey, d c
George Seiler, d c
Jacob Schmidt, d c
Samuel Still, eng'r
Jesse Sutton, s d
John Thompson, dis
Joseph Yocum, alien

SHARPSBURG.

John Sladden, o a
Sylvester Houseman, d c
Thomas H Gibson, minister
Lewis W Lewis, d c
Bostean Kirgner, d c
Lainhart Karl, d c
Jas A Brown, alien, 18 years in country
James C Lewis, s d

George Brawdy, o a
Peter Shultise, o a
H H Lewis, minister
J L Phillips, d c
John J Hanna, d c
Jonathan Clouse, d c
Samuel Clouse, minister
James Saint, d c
Enos Woodruff, minister

Matthew B Brown, d c
Augustus Widman, d c
Joseph Wittman, lost two fingers of right hand
John M Smith, minister
Francis T Gressing, d c
William Conner, pilot
Nicholas Goshorn, d c

M'KEESPORT.

John Stewart, o a
Stewart Smith, d c
John Dixon, d c
B W Rankin, d c
Michael Munhall, d c
Daniel V Day, o a
James E Huey, d c
Uriah Mains, dis
Wm Munkittrick, d c

Geo W Bierly, o a
Wm Fitzgerald, o a
David Miller, d c
Andw J Brown, o a
Robert Haney, o a
John M'Intosh, d c
Jacob Leazer, d c
John Connelly, o a
Henry M'Clockey, d c

Joseph Newell, dis
Geo K Newell, dis
Bernard Winslow, d c
Joseph Cline, d c
William Shaum, d c
Wm B Younker, d c
C C Huey, dis
John Clinelogel, dis

SEWICKLY.

Harlin Hopkins, minister
Chas C M'Connell, t o
Michael Powell, d c
John C Anderson, pilot
S T Kennedy, minister

A B Leonard, minister
E W Gould, n r
Patterson Agree, d c
Samuel J Rankin, d c
Willard Faber, d c
Robert White, minister

Robert E Hopkins, dis
Frank A Meyer, dis
Benj F Peterson, dis
Wm A Adair, dis
C Fletcher Scott, dis

WEST PITTSBURG.

John Camp, d c
Michael Campbell, d c
Fred Figer, d c
Lewis Hoburg, d c
Geo Hass, dis

Michael Hickey, alien
Nicholas Held, alien
Patrick M'Guire, d c
Benj W Stouffer, d c
Thos Stewart, d c

Jno Morgan Stewart, d c
Wm Stewart, d c
John Whalen, alien
Peter Younger, d c

MONONGAHELA.

Aaron Robbin, dis
George Contant, d c

John Sweany, d c
George Murrin, d c

Patrick M'Bride, d c
Peter Lemmon, alien

ELIZABETH.

T S Tower, d c
Abner Peoples, eng'r
John E Shaffer, p m
Robert Stewart, d c

James H Maflett, s d
Samuel Nadler, dis
Alex Matthews, dis
John M'Elhaney, dis

Samuel Hendrickson, pilot
James Elliott, d c
John Carson, dis

WEST ELIZABETH.

Charles Brown, d c
Augustus Snyder, d c

Matthew Laughlin, dis
D Davidson, dis

Isaac B Coates, dis

TOWNSHIPS.

MIFFLIN.

Nicholas Fay, over age
Michael Sosh, d c
James F Calhoun, d c
Conrad Render, d c
Alexander M' Clure, d c
William Morre, d c
Thomas Devie, alien
Timothy Cadman, over age
Charles J. Smyser, d s
George Senker, d c
James Whigam, d c
Christ Distna, dis
James Alnure, dis
Jacob Boyer, over age
Henry Swingler, d c
Phillip Trince, d c
James Clark, d c
Byron Cochran, s d
William Oliver, b c
George Wells, d c
Thomas Clifford, alion
Samuel Parker, alien

Peter Carville, over age
Andrew Large, dis
Robert S Means, d c
Thomas M M'Gorran, d c
John Carns, over age
James Lizesey eng'r
Wm S B Hays, pilot
James Rath, over age
Joseph Livingston, d c
George Pite, alien
Michael Thomas, alien
Walter Walday, alien
John Barner, d c
Robert Barker, alien
John Gross, alien
Peter Hunter, d c
John F Neal, d c
John Haywood. alien
Thomas Sickman, alien
William Collins, alien
Christ Bakerrell, alien
James Wilson, d c

Edward M'Vinna, alien
John M'Gargan, alien
James M'Clure, dis
Conrad Young, d c
John Young, d c
James More, alien
Samual Braddock, alien
Lot Yeats, alien
Michael Deerfecta, dis
Thomas Hadon, dis
Thomas Sharp, d c
Elijah West, d c
John Wosly, d c
Nicholas Coalman, d c
John Carey, alien
David K Calhoun, d c
Robert R Calhoun, d c
John Hamnet, d c
William Cox jr, d c
Casper Meyer, d c
Jacob ortz, alien
John Livingsten, d c

WILKINS.

James Adams, alien
John Baldridge, jr, tel op
Thomas Britton, alien
Matthias Hanisman, dss
Jacob H Jones, ass't p m
Mathew Lawler, alien
Joel Loveridge, dis

Martin Mullooly, d c
Joseph M'Cune, d c
John R Marti, dis
David M'Cune, dis
John M'Cune, dis
Samual A M'Dowell, d c
James H M'Kelvy, p m

Patrick Munhall, alien
John Savage, d c
J D Schooley, d c
Killan Stahl, d c
J M Thomas, minister
D H Toomy, over age
David B Wallace, d c

PITT.

Hugh Atkinson, alien
William Lemon, d c
John Fressel, d c
John Hackinader, discharged
James Yost, discharged
John Murray, d c
George Sheppard, alien
Francis J Weaver, d c
Albert Ingerhart, d c
Charles Wood, over age
Samuel Douglass, discharged
Lewis Manning, d c
Michael Conlin, alien
Joseph Rudge, alien
Thomas J Blerton, d c
Robert Beyty, alien
Richard Sill, over age
David M'Clain, d c
William Green, alien
James Dorly, over age
James M'Vernon. alien
John Vernon. alien
Thomas Barclay, d c
William H Duff, professor
William Metcalf, d c
Thomas Welfer, d c
William Banker, alien
Trovillo May, discharged
James Crosby, d c
James Davis, over age
Francis M'Donald, alien
Anthony Burns, alien
William Moorhead, alien
Alexander A Miller, d c
William Mitchell, d c
David P Estep, school dir
Samuel R Kiemel, d c

Benjamin Kepp, d c
Dennis Kelibe, d c
Thomas Sherridan, d c
Michael O'Connor, alien
Michael Flinn, alien
James Lamont, alien
Hugh Orr, alien
John Grant, alien
William Standing, alien
John Brown, alien
Eirhart Danhorn, d c
William Littsler, alien
Michael Carney, alien
Hezekiah Ruton, d c
John T Wamelink, d c
Isaac Nock, d c
Norris Pyle d c
James M Brown, d c
John M'Curdy, over age
Luster P Chester, pilot
Freeland Chester, pilot
Jacob Taylor, d c
Peter Reniers, d c
Adam Seaman, d c
William Gormly, school dir
Allen Dunn, d c
James Johnston, d c
James M'Alise, discharged
William Birch. d c
Ernest Ritmiller, d c
Samuel D Herron, d c
Henry Kamper, d c
Henry Mitchell, d c
J Ludwig Koethen, d c
James Breen, d c
W A Gildenfenny, d c
James Whiteman. d c
Edward M'Cullum, d c

John Brooks, over age
Robert Arthurs, d c
Joseph Haney, d c
George Ewart, d c
Owen M'Cabe, alien
William J Clark, discharged
William Barton, d c.
William T Hartley, over age
Edward Brooks, discharged
William Murphy, alien
Samuel E Harris, d c
Alexander Black, d c
Robert Cunningham, d c
Bernard Reilley, alien
William J Maguire, discharged
Bernard Lebear, alien
Willian Garman, alien
Owen Carney, discharged
Simon Katy, alien
John Dunlap, over age
Francis L Young, d c
Thomas B Young, over age
John C Cox, d c
Edward Davis, over age
William Evans, over age
William Davis, school dir
William B Evans, discharged
David J Davis, d c
George Hite, d c
James Hughey, d c
William Jones, d c
John Jones, alien
Joseph Nixon, pilot
Joseph Russell, eng'r
Columbus A Ward, dis
James Dugan, non-res
Page Speakman, non-res

ELIZABETH.

Thos Armstrong, alien
Ellis Ball, d c
Jas Barker, alien
John Bishop, alien
Dennis Cuddy, d c
Moses Calhoun, d c
Wm Davis, d c
Richard Davis, alien
John M Daggett, d c
H G Edmundson, d c
James Galloway, d c
James Gillen, d c
Theodore Gilmore, dis
James Howell, dis
Matthew Henderson, jr., d p m
Charles Henderson, alien

Armstrong Hoffman, d c
Michael Hester, over age
Samuel Hardwick, alien
James Hardwick, alien
James Harrison, d c
Philip Hodil, d c
William Thomas, alien
Sam'l Torrence, assistant p m
James Jones, dis
John B Kelly, d c
John J Kingley, dis
Andrew Kelly, d c
Richard Kelly, d c
William Kelly, d c
P A Lytle, d c
Andrew M'Clure, d c
William M'Coy, alien

John W M'Cune, d c
Alexander Miller, alien
Samuel Nolder, dis
Frank Patterson, s d
Daniel Qeery, d c
Matthias Rudolph, d c
John Reynolds, over age
John Rankin, s d
John Riney, dis
William Ray, dis
Hugh Scott, dis
Nathaniel Steer, dis
William Shoaf, d c
Brisbane Wall, dis
John P Willson, d c
James Wiper, dis

VERSAILLES.

James Robinson, d c
Robert Whigman, d c
Joseph Barker, alien, G Wells says he showed naturalization papers and voted on them
William Carter, alien
I G Hickmam, d c
Samuel Stewart, d c
Robert Stewart, d c
John Braidright, over age
James Michaels, d c
William Frederick, d c
Thomas Lynch, alien
John Dods, d c
Henry M'Kee, alien
James M'Kee, alien
Robert Sneddin, alien
Joseph Lehitz, d c
Henry Nickle, d c
Charles Deer, alien
William Deer, d c
James S Jordan, d c
James Westfall, engineer
Michael Marigan, d c
Patrick Conley, d c
Richard H Gray, d c
Benjamin T Cox, engineer

George R Cox, d c
Jonathan Davis, d c
James White, d c
John M'Closkey, d c
Florian Rinehart, d c
James Mitchel, alien
Frank Graham, d c
Francis Cornell, d c
Joseph Perkins, d c
Noah Stahl, d c
Thomas Swan, alien
John Fogle, d c
Jacob Weisen, d c
John Hughey, d c
George Miller, over age
Rush White, d c
Jacob Speelman, d c
James H Kerns, d c
John Snyder, d c
James Mardle, alien
Frederick Grabel, d c
William Smith, d c
William Biddle, d c
David S M'Kee, d c
Frederick Brookmeyer, d c
Conrad Neal, d c
James Chrysta, d c
Thomas Shortley, alien

Mike King, alien
Isaac Peterson, d c
Archy M'Cune, alien
Alexander M'Michaels, d c
John M'Cue, alien
Patrick Green, alien
Philip Boli, engineer
John Davis, d c
Lewis H Near, d c
Michael M'Kenna, over age
Michael Welsh, discharged
Michael Cox, alien
Samuel Kelley, d c
Joseph Ludwick, d c
Andrew Whirling, d c
John Lynch, over age
Samuel J Kerr, d c
Thomas R Kerr, d c
Bernard Hogadon, alien
Alexander Fife, over age
Lockhart Noysmith, d c
William Darling, alien
John Duncan, d c
William Holliday, d c
Jacob Ludwick, d c
James W Taylor, d c
N J Bigley, d c

COLLINS.

Abraham Bolinger, d c
August Bartels, alien
Alfred North, alien
Felix Murray, alien
Reagan Batt, alien
Edward Ashton, d c
Wm Clark, alien
John Cook, alien
Michael Burch, alien
John Bedser, alien
Francis Bissell, d c
William Duff, d c
William Corkay, alien
John Ferguson, alien
James Frankauser, alien
George Fug, alien
Gotlieb Eidenger, alien
Marx Elcessor, alien
Thomas Edwards, alien
William Hocksteen, alien
Peter Gelston, alien
John Gline, alien

John Grouse, alien
James Nesbit, alien
Hugh Newell, alien
Andrew M'Cutcheon, alien
James M'Intyre, alien
George Sliker, alien
Henry Raha, d c
Johnsten Ross, d c
Martin Reigneker, alien
Wallace Radcliffe, d c
David Golden, alien
John Gearing, alien
John Haukel, alien
Charles Holwaden, alien
Nicholas Leech, d c
Harmon Keefer, alien
John Knipper, alien
Michael Callahan, alien
J F Keeler, over age
Thomas Klinefelter, eng'r
William Kepple, alien
Robert Long, c c
Frank Meyer, alien

Michael Moore, alien
J M Little, school director
James Logan, d c
Henry Lagaman, d c
Patrick Laneghan, alien
James Lyons, alien
W S Livingston, minister
John Lowen, over age
J C M'Kelvy, d c
Ephraim Spark, d c
John Perchment, d c
John Petty, alien
John Smith, alien
John G Strubble, d c
James Stree, alien
William Sproul, d c
George Shearer, alien
Julius Shuide, d c
John Barton, d c
Peter Worty, d c
George Youngling, d c
John Mellon, d c

NEVILLE.

Benj Waters, school director
James Jack, d c

Archibald Gibson, s d
Henry Eckert, school director

James Cole, jr., school director
Wm H Seamen, school director

LOWER ST. CLAIR.

James Garghty, d c
John Burford, d c
S T Cuthbert, d c
Wm Golding, an idiot
Thos H Golding, d c
D W C Bidwell, d c
Wm Edwards, alien
Robt Trotter, alien
Wm Beardsley, dis
Jno B Seymore, alien,
Robt Stinson, engineer
Louis Worling, d c
J T Herbert, d c
John Cramer, alien
Wm Armstrong, alien
Peter Kelly, alien

Edward Curran, lunatic
Thos Curran, d c
Max Hageman, leg amputated
Phillip Mertz, d c
Henry Kimmel, d c
Fred Bogeman, alien
Wm Adams, d c
James Miller, alien
Samuel Bruce, alien
Henry Backer, alien
Simon J Turburg, alien
Alex Hilderbran, d c
J Jones, d c
Wm L Toland, ass't p m
John Lutz, s d
D Cunningham, over age

Joseph Keeling, d c
Joseph Mahler, d c
Jas Wightman, alien
Wm Hartung, d c
Daniel Griffin, d c
Frank Armryan, d c
George W Chambers, d c
Louis Tiernan, d c
Peter Barok, d c
Jacob Hasenfratz, d c
Michael M'Swiggen, over age
John Harvey, d c
Frank Rogers, d c
Neal O'Neal, alien
Alfred Shettle, d c
Gregor Hide, d c

PEEBLES.

A H Gross, s d
David Carmichael, alien
Philip Cash, d c
James Burke, alien
John Grey, d c
Henry Strothoff, alien
John Wessen, alien
Henry Schnellbach, alien
George Holler, d c
John Moore, alien
George Buck, d c

Lemuel Spahr, d c
James Duval, alien
Anthony Duval, alien
John Scanlon, alien
John Schmidt, alien
Peter Lightenthal, alien
William A Burchfield, min
John Hannager, alien
Gilber Turner, alien
Robert Patterson, s d
James Murdock, d c

Jacob McAlister, alien
Frederick Nedhamer, d c
Alfred Harrison, d c
Louis Calmet, alien
Claude Budget, alien
John Bruce, alien
William Wylie, s d
John Lepro, alien
Hill Burgwin, d c
George Buck, d c

SNOWDEN.

Joseph Maits, d c
Thomas J Snee, d c
John H Sowderbach, d c
A G Simpson, d c
Wm Glen, d c
Oliver Sheets, d c
William Cowan, d c
Jas W Skees, d c
Jno M'Clain, d c

John Maits, jr, d c
George Bayer, d c
Leonard P Bayer, d c
John Lafferty, d c
L M' C Larimer, d c
Joseph Young, d c
William Snee, d c
J J Miller, d c
H L Marshall, s d
J D Murray, d c

Wm Woods, d c
Wm Boyer d c
John Sickman, d c
D C Hultz, d c
E A Wood, d c
Robert E M' Corkle, d c
P R Boyer, d c
David M' Alister, d c
Leonard Boyer, d c

M'CLURE.

Alexander Wadlow, sr., dis
Alfred Wall, dis
Henry Beeker, d c
Rufus Brandon, over age
William J Beatty, alien

C Coleman, s d
Adam Craft, alien
Jacob Frantz, s d
Michael Foulk, d c
C Gerber, over age
Thomas Hughes, s d

Daniel Lecy, alien
Thomas Madden, d c
James Old, s d
William Potter, over age
William Scothorn, d c

RICHLAND.

William Dickey, d c
John Nosser, d c

Andrew Staley, d c
Thomas Staley, d c

Samuel Dickson, d c
John M'Caw, d c

INDIANA.

Robert H Wills, s d	Samuel M'Pherron, d c	John Henderson, p m
Alexander Whitten, d c	David M'Clelland, d c	Francis Stroud, d c
Peter Seiferd d c	Samuel Mareshall, d c	Oliver P Henderson, d c
James Tirrell, d c	James Lemmon, d c	Matthew C Crawford, d c
Jacob W Thompson, d c	David Jones, alien	James C Campbell, d c
Phillip Skillen, alien	Frederick Hodil, d c	John Cable, d c
Wm Robinson, d c	Philip Hodil, d c	Edward Cable, d c
James Robinson, d c	Philip Hodil, d c	Dennis Cook, alien
James G Prigby, d c	John Hodil, d c	Wm Barkley, d c
Peter Quinette, d c	Ezekiel Gordon, pilot	David Boreland, d c
Alfred Quinette, d c	John Hutchison, over age	John B Beatty, s d
Thos D Patterson, en e	William Hart, d c	Alexander Bovard, d c
Absolem Pettigrew, d c	Joseph A Hancock, d c	Josoph Bestler, alien
Wm Noble, alien	Peter Hutchison, d c	

SHALER.

John Elder, d c	James Campbell, d c	Michael Ritticer, d c
Levi Wetsel, d c	Samuel Campbell, d c	Andrew M'Feran
Christopher Distler, over age	Robert Miller, d c	Michael Lebald, d c
Charles Newmaster, d c	Cleman Tanner, d c	Conrad King, d c
John Bradshaw, alien	Henry Frederick, d c	John Herron, over age
Harrison Wible, d c	Joseph Fogel, d c	Jacob Barr, alien
Thomas D Stone, d c	Peter Fernof, d c	Michael Milbert, d c
Leonctious Bullion, d c	Robert Thompson, school dir	Levi Milbert, d c
John Bullion, d c	D Thompson, over age	Hamilton Beatty, arsenal
John Hoon, d c	John G Zimmerman, d c	

JEFFERSON.

Josiah Aber, school director	Peter Huffman, alien	Christopher Stokes, alien
Milton Bedell, d c	Irwin Hamilton, d c	Adam Shatz, d c
John Boyd, deserter	Thomas Gelitely, alien	John Sheplar, school director
John Cadick, alien	Frederick Luits, d c	Robert Taylor, alien
Isaac B Coats, discharged	William Loutlit, alien	Henry Whitaker, d c
Edward Stokes, alien	A Gilbert Kirtland, d c	Reuben White, d c
David Davis, d c	Edwin Oudy, d c	Joseph Wilson, d c
William Fortune, d c	Samuel Roberts, d c	Thomas Wakefield, d c
Henry Devore, d c	William Roy, d c	Peter Dersam, d c
	Harvey H Stewart, d c	

RESERVE.

William Marshel, d c	Michael Walter, alien	Xavier Lander, d c
Gotlieb Hangstoter, d c	John Hartung, d c	August Jeckel, d c
William Stimple, d c	Adam Fath, d c	Lorentz Walter, d c
Henry C Reineman, d c	Daniel Hahmen, alien	George Hetzel, d c
Joseph Schmidt, d c	Henry Steffler, d c	Louis Schad, d c
Henry Vogel, d c	I Birchel, con scruples	John Kunkel, alien
	Gottlieb G Mayer, d c	

CRESCENT.

Robert Brotherton, d c	William Hahn, d c	Frank M'Clelland, d c
William Creighton, s d	William Harper, s d	John Russell, s d
Isaac P Dunlap, d c	James M'Namee, d c	Christopher Shefler, d c

BALDWIN.

John Agnew, over age
John Benton, d c
John Bakewell, alien
Valentine Betz, d c
William Bennett, d c
Wm Crouch, d c
Watson Craft, over age
Edward Davis, alien
John Veal, d c
Joseph Drake, d c
Benj Elliott, d c
Henry Eltenham, d c
Ferdinand Farrier, alien

Wm Fawks, over age
George Goodboy, d c
John Grass, d c
John Griffith, over age
James Gibbs, d c
John F Wicks, d c
George Huey, d c
Benj Hunter, d c
Jacob Honing, d c
Henry B Long, d c
James Moore, over age
Jacob May, d c
Jas M'Fadden, over age

James M'Anulty, d c
Henry J Ortman, d c
John Peach, jr, d c
John B Plappard, d c
Michael Ripple, d c
Wm Ripka, alien
Sidney Stewart, en e
Jacob Spirt, d c
Henry Shemik, dis
Matthew Schide, over age
Fred Travers, alien
Henry Voight, d c

MOON.

Gilbert G Gordon, d c
Robert Hood, d c
Philip H Stevenson, school dir
Levi Stevenson, post master
James Aten, d c
John M'Cutcheon, d c
David Harper, d c
Benjamin B Slay, d c
William Q Shrodes, pilot
James Ramsey, d c

John Creighton, d c
Frank Eberly, d c
William J Backhouse, d c
Samuel Oustot, d c
James M'Miller, d c
Samuel J Ewing, dep p m
P S Jennings, d c
John Thompson, alien
Thomas H M'Clelland, p m
William Perry M'Cabe, d c

George Seibert, d c
William F Stoddart, d c
William K Nesbit, school dir
William Ewing, dep p m
James Guy, d c
Isaac N deemer, d c
Robert Parker, d c
John C Harper, d c
James White, d c
William Bickerstaff, d c

UNION.

Alexander Adamson, alien
George Archbold, alien
David Cooper, alien
John Cromby, alien
James Carter, jr, d c
William M Carter, d c

Joseph Fleming, engineer
William Frew, school director
William Linton, alien
E G D Mayes, d c
Wilson Ramsey, d c
George Rous, d c

Francis Rodgers, d c
Thos Silk, d c
William J Shedden, engineer
David Singleton, engineer
Andrew Williamson, alien
Robert Miller, alien

SOUTH FAYETTE.

Matthias Manuel, over age
William Nicholson, d c
Thomas Herron, d c
Martin Dolen, d c
David Gilmore, school dir

James Quinn, secrt'd from dep
T F M'Cabe, d c
William Carson, alien
Jacob Richards, d c
William Hammond, alien

J M Shane, d c
James R Dinsmore, d c
Randolph Clark, d c
James Mawhiney, d c
John Patterson, d c

M'CANDLESS.

James Wallace, d c
David R Moore, eng'r
Benjamin Willoughby, d c
Conrad Emeric, d c

John Shanky, d c
Francis Koomer, eng'r
Frederick Nuhn, d c
Philip Sarver, d c

James Sarver, d c
Jacob Sarver, d c
Daniel Willoughby, d c

SEWICKLY.

James Newell, alien

Jacob Jost, d c
Elias Reno, school director

Samuel Sawer, school dir

FINLAY.

Henry Strouss, d c
Jackson Howard, d c
John M Stewart, s d
William James Porter, d c
Joseph Soringer, d c
John Stewart, d e
Robert M'Eyeal, school dir
Thomas F Jeffery, d c
Joseph M'Elheny, d c
George Springer, d c
James Bingham, asst p m
Samuel J Byers, d c

Samuel S Meanor, d c
James Dixson, d c
James S Oliver, d c
John L Stevenson, d c
James D M'Bride, d c
William V Hays, school dir
James B M'Bride, d c
John M Lewis, d c
Montgomery Gordon, d c
James D M'Carther, d c
William S Wilson, d c
John Ackleson, d c
Thomas B M'Bride, d c

Samuel M'Bride, d c
Fulton Custer, d c
Thomas Burns, d c
James A M'Null, school dir
Richard D Stewart, d c
James R Stewart, d c
George Burns, d c
John Harper, d c
A D Burns, school director
John Doughty, d c
William S Linton, d c
Levi W Steuenson, d c

ROBINSON.

John A M'Kee, d c
James Edmundson, d c
Alexander Ewing, d c
James H Dick, d c
Michael Leonard, post master
Ewing M'Kown, d c
Jacob Allen, d c
Michael Woods, alien
Edward Johnston, alien
William Caughey, d c
Robert F Gibson, d c

Theodore Phillips, d c
Johnston Stephenson, d c
Andrew Smith, d c
Samuel Glass, s d
Thomas Wood, d c
Samuel S Glass, d c
Patrick Duffy, d c
Jacob Clever, d c
William Hill, d c
William Young, d c
David Gibson, d c

Samuel Thornsbury, d c
George Geiser, d c
Andrew M'Farland, over age
Andrew Clever, d c
Lewis D Mitchell, d c
John Holmes, d c
William Ewing, d c
John Clark, d c
Michael Joice, alien
Joseph M'Curdy, d c

PLUM.

Robt Black, over age
John A Conner, p m
Hugh Donnel, d c
Wm Grabner, over age
W W Jones, dis

A A Kuhn, dis
Wm M'Laughlin, d c
Alexander M'Math, d c
H Reiter, blind of an eye
Hugh M'Craddy, d c
Andrew Kerr, d c

John S Stewart, s d
W K Stewart, s d
Jackson Aber, s d
Jas H Kearns, d c
Phillip Bigley, m c

EAST DEER.

Jas Henderson, school director
Mark Marvin, d c
Archibald Pillow, s d
John Raymond, discharged

George G Reimer, d c
Andrew Reimer, d c
Jacob Huddle, d c
Samuel Robertson, s d

Robert Speer, discharged
Jas Hazlett, school director
Henry Ellman, d c

ROSS.

James S Cable, d c
George Peterman, d c

John J Henderson, eng'r
William Ray, school director
William Cable, d c

William Fairfield, d c
Henry Cable, d c

WEST DEER.

John Campbell, d c

William Hamilton, d c
John P Conley, d c

Robert Conley, d c

NORTH FAYETTE.

William Herron, s d
David Johnston, d c
Abraham Bell, over age
Matthew A M'Gregor, d c
George Thompsen, dis
D M Cannon, d c
Samual M'Coy, d c
Samual Stevenson, d c
Joseph Lindsey, d c
Alfred C Rineman, d c
Joseph Rineman, d c
Thompson Jeffrey, d c
J P Hughes, d c

John Fulton, d c
Wm C M Farland, d c
Robert M'Farland, asst p m
Richard L Morrow, d c
Cyrus R Potter, minister
Samual Cavitt, d c
William H Clark, d c
John Whitman, d c
Oliver M'Lean, d c
Alex W Morrow, d c
Adam Potter, d c
Isaac J Stewart, d c
Jas M Lewis, d c

M' Crea M' Whister, d c
John M'Leastor, alien
Gabriel Walker, d c
Josiah Walker, d c
Ezekiel Walker, d c
Joseph R Farmer, d c
Joseph Wallace, d c
John H Miller, d c
George M M'Kee, d c
John Tracy, alien
Alex Allison, d c
Thomas R Partridge, d c

OHIO.

Jacob Gass d c
Harrison Grubs, d c
Cunningham Snickle, alien
John Curns, alien
Samuel M'Cory, d c
George Fagains, d c

Robert Crawford, d c
William Crawford, d c
William M Dean, alien
Cornelius Smith, d c
Daniel Snider, d c
John Lindsey, d c

Thomas Thompson, alien
Aaron Grubs, s d
Samuel Schyler, d c
Jacob Crees, d c
Samuel Cress, d c
Abraham Fulkman, d c

FRANKLIN.

Jacob Fisher, d c
G H Wallace, school director
George Sickels, d c
George Berger, d c
Samuel Wilson, d c
Thomas Robinson, d c

David Forsyth, d c
John Fry, d c
Alexander Forsyth, d c
Phillip Fry, school director
Edward Thompson, d c
John Frazier, d c

Wm Neely, school director
John Smith, d c
Jas Neely, school director
Samuel Neely, d c
James Sewright, d c

UPPER ST. CLAIR.

Robert Rankin, discharged
Samuel Morton, discharged
David Higbee, school director
James Fife, d c

William Roach, school director
David Donaldson, d c
Thomas M'Millan, d c
Andrew M'Millan, d c

W J Gilmore, school director
James Duff, d c
Thomas Duff, d e

PINE.

Richard H Pearce, s d
John Dean, d c

John Campbell, d c
Robert Campbell, d c
John Ross, d c

James Stoup, s d
John Rigby, d c

HAMPTON.

Alexander Speer, d c
Robert Chigeman, d c

James M'Caw, d c
Joseph R Hart, d c

Robert Scott, d c

PENN.

Samuel M'Manus, dis
Henry M'D Morrow, s d

John G M'Cabe, d c
Whitmer Stoner, d c

Joseph Huey, s d

FAWN.

John J Warner, dis
James A Smith, d c
Thomas J Stevenson, p m
John Pratt, dis
Patrick Parcell, alien

Patrick M'Merrell, alien
William S Jones, d c
John Esler, d c
Michael Carmody, alien
Thomas Coyle, alien

William T Anderson, d e
John C Anderson, dis
Samuel C Alter, s d
Joseph Burmaster, assist p m
Francis Brown, alien

SCOTT.

Charles Lyster, dis
Casper Anay, alien

John A. Irwin, dis
George Cobbet, alien

Lafayette Lea, dis
Isaac Hultz, dis

CHARTIERS.

Adolph Ager, d c
Levi Spreity, d c

Wm Barnes, d c
John Snyder, d c

John Hags, alien

PATTON.

Robert Cloyston, school dir

David Gill, d c
James Long, d c

George Linn, d c

www.ingramcontent.com/pod-product-compliance
Lightning Source LLC
Chambersburg PA
CBHW021531270326
41930CB00008B/1192